The
Lovebird
Handbook

Vera Appleyard

With Full-color Photographs

BARRON'S

Acknowledgments

For Clara and Fred, my parents, who always encouraged me to write. Special thanks to Nancy Porras for sharing her exceptional knowledge.

About the Author

Vera Appleyard has raised a variety of color mutations of peachfaced lovebirds for many years. She also raises Fischer's and Abyssinian lovebirds. She is the Guide for Pet Birds at *About.com* and owner of the popular lovebird website, *ParrotParrot.com*. She has an MFA in Dramatic Writing from New York University and works as a writer in Los Angeles.

Cover Photos

Front cover: Joan Balzarini (large photo, bottom left, bottom right); Matthew Vriends (top right, middle). Back cover: Joan Balzarini (large photo); Matthew Vriends (inset). Inside front and back covers: B. Everett Webb.

Photo Credits

Vera Appleyard: 36, 83. Joan Balzarini: viii, 12, 57, 73, 84, 93 (bottom), 96 (bottom), 117. Brockman/Wiching: 115. R. Erhart: 15, 102 (bottom), 103 (top). Ardea Fink: 4 (top). Okapia/Durk: 2. Reinhardt: 101 (top, bottom), 129. Scholtz: 103 (bottom), 104 (top), 105.
All other photos by B. Everett Webb.

© Copyright 2001 by Barron's Educational Series, Inc.

All inquiries should be addressed to:
Barron's Educational Series, Inc.
250 Wireless Boulevard
Hauppauge, New York 11788
http://www.barronseduc.com

International Standard Book No. 0-7641-1827-7

Library of Congress Catalog Card No. 2001037360

Library of Congress Cataloging-in-Publication Data

Appleyard, Vera.
   The lovebird handbook / Vera Appleyard.
      p. cm.
   ISBN 0-7641-1827-7
   1. Lovebirds. I. Title.

SF473.L6 A66 2001
636.6'864—dc21   2001037360

Printed in Hong Kong
9 8 7 6 5 4 3

Important Note

The subject of this book is how to take care of lovebirds in captivity. In dealing with these birds, always remember that newly purchased birds—even when they appear perfectly healthy—may well be carriers of salmonella. This is why it is advisable to have a new bird wellness examination performed by an avian veterinarian and to observe strict hygienic rules. Other infectious diseases that can endanger humans, such as psittacosis, ornithosis, and tuberculosis, occasionally occur in psittacine birds. If you see a doctor because you or a member of your household has symptoms of a cold or of the flu, mention that you keep birds. No one who is allergic to feathers or feather dust should keep birds. If you have any doubts, consult your physician before you buy a bird.

Contents

Preface

The nine species of *Agapornis* comprise a diverse group of fascinating and colorful African parrots known collectively as lovebirds. These birds have long delighted pet bird owners. Their inquisitive, playful nature and small size make hand-raised lovebirds ideal pets. This book will guide you in how best to choose a quality lovebird, as well as give solid advice on how to care for and train your bird so it will be a happy, well-adjusted pet. If you already have a lovebird and it has developed such bad habits as biting or constant screaming, there are tips on how to work on turning these behaviors around, as well as how to prevent them with any future birds you might own. You will learn how focused observation of your bird and its behaviors can help you reinforce positive behaviors and sounds, while not inadvertently encouraging any negative behavior or noise. The chapter on breeding and hand-feeding will help the beginner start a breeding program with a solid foundation. The book also includes tips on diet and nutrition, how to recognize the early signs of illness, and a primer on the rules of color inheritance. Whether you are considering the purchase of your first pet parrot, working with a current pet lovebird, or getting ready to start breeding and raising pet-quality babies, this book will guide you in the best care of these captivating birds.

A yellow Fischer's split lutino.

Chapter One

Agapornis: The Jewels of Africa

Natural History

Lovebirds have long fascinated people both in the wild and in captivity. The first image conjured up when most people think about these birds is of a pair snuggling closely together on a branch. Their tendency to sit in pairs mutually preening each other led to the genus name *Agapornis,* which comes from the Greek *agape* (love) and *ornis* (birds). The French call them *les inseperables,* or the inseparables, a further testament to their affectionate nature. While affection between compatible pairs can be a joy to watch, lovebirds can be quite territorial and will defend their nest and living space against other lovebirds of the same or different species. Understanding their basic nature will help pet owners and breeders create the most harmonious home possible for these delightful birds.

From the woodlands of the island of Madagascar to the coastal plains

The tendency of the Agapornis *species to cuddle in pairs is why they were given the common name lovebirds.*

of Southwest Africa, north to the highlands of Ethiopia dwell the nine species of lovebird, each in its own distinct geographical area. Lovebirds are parrots. This often comes as a surprise to those investigating the possibility of purchasing one as a pet. The hooked beak and the zygodactyl feet (two toes face forward, two backward) are characteristics of the Psittaciformes order of birds. Because they are parrots, they have the ability to mimic, although they are not as famous for this ability as are budgerigars, African grey parrots, and Amazon parrots. The genus *Agapornis* comprises nine genetically and geographically distinct species. Seven of these fit into two basic groups. The eye-ring species include masked, Fischer's, Nyasa, and black-cheeked lovebirds. The sexually dimorphic species include Abyssinian, Madagascar, and red-faced lovebirds. Two species fall into their own distinct groups: the peach-faced lovebird and the Swindern's or Swinderen's lovebird.

The general characteristics of the genus are a small, stocky build with

Wild Fischer's lovebirds, as well as many other lovebird species, often raid crops of corn.

Doing so creates hybrids, a bird that is neither one species nor the other. Because of strict rules on importation of wild-caught specimens of *Agapornis,* the various species must be kept separate and distinct or we run the risk of losing a true wild-type specimen in aviculture.

The first lovebirds were brought to Europe during the eighteenth century when exploration of Africa by Europeans began to reach its peak. Europeans delighted in the brightly colored, chattering pairs of lovebirds.

Lovebirds as Pets Today

Parrots were kept as pets and aviary birds in ancient Greece and Rome. One of the most famous early keepers of parrots was Alexander the Great. These delightful and intelligent birds have found their homes in royal courts and presidential homes. They were given as gifts to kings and emperors and traded by explorers throughout the world. Humans are drawn to their ability to mimic and their tendency to entertain with comical antics.

Lovebirds continue to delight pet owners in contemporary society. The development of commercial hand-feeding formulas has made it possible for breeders to raise tame, sweet pets that make a welcome addition to the household. These birds have a distinct, high-pitched

a short, blunt tail and a beak that is proportionally large for their body size. Eight of the species come from the mainland of Africa. The ninth, Madagascar lovebirds, hail from the island of Madagascar off the eastern coast of southern Africa.

The nine species are separated in the wild by geography. For this reason, they should not be interbred.

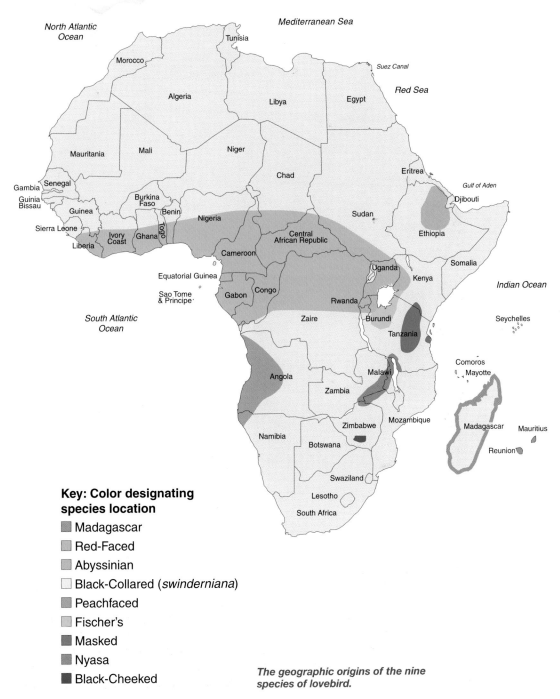

Key: Color designating species location

- ▢ Madagascar
- ▢ Red-Faced
- ▢ Abyssinian
- ▢ Black-Collared (*swinderniana*)
- ▢ Peachfaced
- ▢ Fischer's
- ▢ Masked
- ▢ Nyasa
- ▢ Black-Cheeked

The geographic origins of the nine species of lovebird.

3

A pair of Nyasa lovebirds inspect a potential nesting site.

Peachfaced lovebird in the wild-type coloration.

A hand-tamed blue mutation of the peachfaced lovebird.

All four birds are peachfaced lovebirds in the color mutations of cobalt, blue, creamino, and dark green.

call that is rarely offensive to people. Their small size makes them ideal apartment pets. Tame lovebirds do well as single pets, dispelling the myth that these birds cannot thrive unless kept in pairs. Although a frightened, untamed lovebird can deliver a strong bite, it cannot do the damage a larger parrot such as an Amazon or macaw could do with its powerful beak.

Later I will discuss in detail the wide variety of color mutations in African lovebirds. However, understanding some basic information about this is important before continuing. Many people recognize the term peachfaced lovebird but do not fully realize that other mutations of lovebirds that belong to this same species are still peachfaced lovebirds, even if their particular mutation has resulted in the reduction or elimination of the peachface. For example, a Dutch blue lovebird is a par-blue mutation of a peachfaced lovebird. Other names you may hear are cinnamon, lutino, creamino, violet, slate, pied, or opaline. This is also the case with other species of lovebirds in whom a wide variety of mutated colors have been developed over years of captive breeding. A blue-masked lovebird is simply a blue

mutation of a black-masked lovebird. They are still the same species. Although the visual differences between an albino Fischer's lovebird and a wild-type Fischer's are dramatic, they are the same species.

A variety of mutations of peachfaced lovebirds in a large aviary flight.

Lovebirds in Aviaries

Lovebirds come in a wide variety of color mutations, making them beautiful aviary birds. It is best to stick to one species within a single flight, however, due to the aggressiveness that often occurs between the different species. While a single lovebird can rarely make enough noise to rouse the neighbors, an aviary full of these chattering parrots can raise an eyebrow or two. Therefore, taking this noise into consideration is important before starting an outdoor aviary with more than a few pairs of lovebirds.

Exhibition Lovebirds

Lovebirds have been a part of aviculture for many decades now. The development of such stunning mutations as lutino and albino, to name a few, has led to the establishment of organized groups of fanciers who travel the country and even the world to exhibit their lovebirds. Judges base awards on a bird's size, conformation, comportment, color, and general appearance. Winning the top bench in such an exhibition can dramatically increase the value of birds in that family line as well as the reputation of the breeder. Exhibitors prepare for the season by making sure their birds get sufficient exercise to develop the breast area properly. They will also allow the bird to practice for a show by having it spend some time in the regulation show cage. A winning bird needs to be calm yet alert.

Anyone hoping to begin a top-notch breeding program would do well to consider purchasing their initial stock from breeders who belong to international societies dedicated to the *Agapornis* species. However, do not expect to start with top-bench

A prize-winning lutino peachfaced lovebird in a regulation show cage.

birds. These exhibition-quality lovebirds can be prohibitively expensive. You can, through careful study and mentorship under an experienced breeder, buy a few top birds from these breeders then carefully select babies from these pairs who have the most desirable characteristics. After breeding this way for a number of generations, you can often develop your own top-bench line of lovebirds.

Chapter Two

Picking a Pet

Main Considerations

Whether you look for local breeders or visit pet stores in your area, the most important qualities to look for in a pet lovebird are good health and a friendly personality. Bird owners often say, "The bird picked me." This statement contains quite a bit of truth. Sometimes you will feel an instant bond with a particular bird. It might be the way it cocks its head to look at you or how it chirps to be let out of the cage when it sees you walk by.

A frightened, biting bird might calm down, but you will certainly be way ahead of the game if you pick a lovebird who already enjoys being handled. While the bird might be nervous with you at first because you are a stranger, it should at least appear comfortable with the breeder or current caretaker. One of the most common complaints I hear is that the seller claimed a wild, terrified bird would calm down with a

A healthy lovebird has bright eyes, a strong stance, clear nares, and a well-developed breast area.

few days of handling, yet months later the bird seems as intractable as ever. The best choice for a pet will always be the bird who is already quite tame and amenable to handling by humans.

Pet Stores

If you plan to purchase a lovebird at a pet store, visit the store a number of times first. Look for signs of sick birds, dirty cage conditions, and poor diet. If the store smells bad, the workers do not know the difference between a lovebird and a cockatiel, and the birds have only dirty water and a bowl of seeds in the cage, you will want to look elsewhere. Be sure you go to the store a few times. Birds do soil their water quickly, so to be fair, dirty water may actually have been clean just an hour before you arrived. However, if the water has film on it or is filled with rotting food, this is not a good sign.

Breeders

Many people have found buying a lovebird directly from a breeder to be best. You often get much better advice because an experienced breeder will usually be much more knowledgeable about the care of

Play areas and cages in pet stores should appear clean and well-maintained.

lovebirds than a pet store worker who only sees them occasionally. Getting species-specific advice is

always preferable to getting generic parrot advice. Another issue with store-bought birds is that pet stores usually have birds from a variety of sources. Babies from different aviaries are often mixed together, increasing the risk of disease transmission should any one bird be sick.

Closed Aviaries

Do not be put off by closed aviaries. This is when breeders do not allow outsiders into the aviary areas. They will bring a baby out to you so you can see if this is a bird you might like. They will not allow you into the breeding areas or any areas where younger babies might be housed. This is an excellent practice because it protects their birds from disease and stress.

Breeder Qualifications

Many lovebird breeders belong to international societies dedicated to lovebirds or parrots in general. This often shows a dedication to the conservation of the species and proper avicultural practices. By joining such an organization, these breeders show an interest in learning more about the species they breed. They will often band each bird with traceable society bands that give their initials and the year the bird hatched.

Adopting a Lovebird

Another option is to adopt an older lovebird. Make sure the person selling or giving the bird up for adoption has a good reason. You do not want to adopt a bird with behavioral and health problems unless you are fully prepared to incur the expense and time necessary to remedy the situation. Some good reasons a person might need to give up a bird could be moving to a pet-free building, allergies, changes in their lives that give them little time to spend with the pet, and the illness or death of the original owner. However, if the bird is not tame, do not fail to realize taming an older bird set in its ways can be a difficult if not impossible task. Some people seem to have a gift for taming such birds, but you need to ask yourself if you are one of these people before taking on this responsibility.

The Myth About Pairs

Many people, even pet store owners, believe the myth that lovebirds must be kept in pairs. While seeing two lovebirds cuddling on a perch is certainly heartwarming, they will not pine away and die without a mate. This is particularly true if you get a tame lovebird bonded to humans. Generally a tame, hand-fed lovebird that has recently weaned will transfer its bond to the new owner very quickly. When a young bird is still in the presence of the breeder or its siblings, the bird may seem more interested in them. However, as soon as it realizes you are now its flock, a socialized bird will quickly come around.

While it is a sweet sight to see two lovebirds cuddle on a branch, it is a myth that a single lovebird will die without a mate.

Weaned vs. Unweaned

Another persistent and patently false belief is that a bird you hand-feed yourself will make a better pet than one weaned by the breeder or pet store. There is absolutely no need to buy an unweaned baby lovebird, especially if you have never hand-fed a bird. The risks you take in doing this without adequate training far outweigh the benefits of being the mama bird. A just-weaned, well-socialized baby lovebird will transfer its bond to the new owner within a matter of days,

A well-socialized lovebird will quickly transfer its bond to a new owner.

sometimes even in a few hours. As long as it feels safe and has a good home environment, it will calm down and accept you as the new flock.

The dangers of an inexperienced person hand-feeding a baby lovebird can lead to tragedy or very high veterinarian bills. Some of the risks are formula that is too hot and that burns the crop, formula that is too cold and causes sour or slow crop, aspirated formula that causes pneumonia or death, and undernourishment of the bird that causes health or development problems. If you are not familiar with the needs of the species and such variables as the maximum acceptable weight loss during weaning, you can easily harm or kill a baby bird.

One of the best ways to get a truly tame, sweet pet lovebird is to reserve one that is currently being hand-fed. You can then pick up the bird once the breeder or pet store has fully weaned it. Begin handling your lovebird on a daily basis and it will quickly transfer the bond to you.

Hand-fed Is Not Enough

While hand-feeding is an excellent way to raise a tame, loveable pet, it is only the beginning of socializing a lovebird. Most breeders of these species know that handling the bird between feedings, especially when they near fledgling age (six weeks), is an essential part of socializing an essentially wild creature. The more a young bird is handled, pet, and spoken to during the formative months, the more sociable and flexible it will be. In fact, this type of consistent socialization needs to be maintained for the first six months of the bird's life. Lovebirds not handled on a daily basis early on will often revert to their wild nature, although this tendency can vary dramatically from bird to bird. I have found that lovebirds' personalities are as distinct from one bird to the next as are personalities among people. Some birds are brave, some shy; some birds are bold, some tentative. Picking a bird whose personality suits you is best. If a very playful, active bird would strain your patience, choose a more laid-back, cuddly bird.

The method of hand-feeding can also impact the personality and socialization of the bird. Some breeders power feed their birds, which is a fast plunge of the syringe to fill them up quickly, then put them back into the brooder with little or no interaction. These birds can revert quickly to their wild nature. The more a bird is handled during the formative weeks and months of its life, the more tame it will remain. Knowing when the bird was weaned is also important. While lovebirds do fledge in the wild at around six weeks of age, parents continue to supplement their diet by feeding them directly on occasion. They do not simply kick their babies out of the nest at six weeks and send them off on their own. Most parrot species

A tame black-masked lovebird learns to step up.

continue to feed their young for a period of time after they have fledged. In fact, some of the larger cockatoo species supplement their babies' diets for four or five months. Hand-fed lovebirds should be allowed to wean on their own schedule. This can vary from 7 to 11 weeks. Birds that are abundance weaned[1] in this manner tend to be more secure and have a good time period in which to learn to eat a variety of foods while still getting the comforting and nutritious supplements of warm formula. There is no

---

[1]The conecpt of *abundance weaning* is trademarked by Phoebe Greene Linden, Santa Barbara Bird Farm, Santa Barbara, CA 93108. *http://www.santabarbarabirdfarm.com*

need to create anxiety in a young bird by forcing it to meet its own nutritional needs on some predetermined date.

Lovebirds are extremely curious and intelligent creatures. They are also flock creatures. Their inherent need is to be part of a group. When you become the flock, consistent handling and socialization of your bird will reinforce positive interaction. Many people believe you should not handle the bird for the first few days in the new home to give the bird a chance to adjust to the new environment. Just the opposite is true. Handling your bird for short periods off and on during the first few days will help it adjust to you and its new home. However, you must do this in a quiet room where not much activity is occurring, as the bird will be very nervous when first settling into its new home. Move slowly, talk in a calming voice, and make sure no one is going to run into the room suddenly during these initial periods when you handle your new pet.

A Big Parrot in a Small Package

One of the questions often heard by prospective parrot owners is, "What is a good starter bird?" There is no such thing as a starter bird. They all require similiar care and training. One of the great aspects of keeping lovebirds as pets is the fact that they can be very similar to larger parrots yet are much easier to house. They have the curiosity, intelligence, and playfulness that you see in larger parrot species. They can be as willful as an Amazon and as cuddly as a cockatoo. You need to approach these birds the same way you do larger parrots. This means using the same training and socialization techniques you would with any bird in this class. They are not low-maintenance parrots just because they are small. They need as much interaction, play, exercise, and training as their larger counterparts to remain calm and enjoyable pets.

Male vs. Female

The most popular pet lovebird species are not sexually dimorphic. This means you cannot simply look at a peachfaced, masked, or Fischer's lovebird and know its sex. The only exception is when you have a bird that carries a sex-linked mutation and you know which parent carried this particular gene (see Chapter 9 on genetics). Because of this, purchasing a specific sex is not easy, although some breeders will do a DNA test for an extra charge if you are set on a male or female. While birds near a year of age can show certain signs or behaviors that indicate sex, this is not always reliable. Even the most experienced lovebird breeders have difficulty determining sex during the first few months of a lovebird's life.

Three male red-faced lovebirds share a perch.

Male lovebirds do have a reputation for being easier to keep tame and less likely to bite. However, female lovebirds can make extremely good pets. In fact, in my experience, female lovebirds kept singly as pets are more likely to talk than are male lovebirds.

For both sexes, some hormone issues can come into play when the bird reaches maturity. For males, this can be regurgitating for the owner whom they consider the mate. They will often rub themselves on perches and toys as well. This is harmless behavior. However, some people are bothered by it, especially if the bird seems to act out these sexual behaviors obsessively. Hens determined to breed will sometimes lay eggs on the bottom of the cage and become territorial. This is an instinct to protect the nest. Some measures can be taken to prevent this from getting out of hand. A good idea is to have a cage with a grated bottom to keep hens separated from the lining. Otherwise, they may use these materials to build a nest in the cage. Giving a hen a sleeping hut or other hiding area is also not a good idea because they will often turn this into a nest and can become very aggressive in protecting this territory.

Spring tends to be the time when sexual behavior increases. Many pet bird keepers will cover the cage with a dark, bird-safe cover in the evening and remove it when they wake in the morning. This ensures that the bird gets plenty of dark sleep and can also simulate the shorter hours of winter, thus short-circuiting the mating cycle. By making sure the bird gets 10 to 12 hours of dark sleep time, you can often reduce springtime hormonal behavior.

Lovebirds of both sexes can make excellent pets if the proper steps are taken to keep your bird tame and socialized. This means creating a strong bond where you are in charge and giving consistent cues so your bird understands the rules. Cage territoriality can be dramatically reduced by always using the *step-up* command when removing your lovebird from the cage. This is preferable to allowing the bird to

If you give a single pet bird, particularly a hen, or a pair of pet birds any type of sleeping box or nest, you may inadvertently encourage breeding.

wander out on its own. These issues will be discussed in more detail in Chapter 6, "Behavior and Training."

Finding Quality Birds

Personal references from other owners of lovebirds can be an excellent way to find a quality bird for a pet. If you already have a relationship with a veterinarian for other pets, you can ask him or her to recommend a particular breeder. Many veterinarians have regular clients who breed birds, and they will have a good sense of who uses proper avicultural practices and raises quality birds.

The worst thing you can do is decide to buy a lovebird on impulse. Do not buy a bird just because you feel sorry for it sitting in a cage at the pet store. By educating yourself, you will not make the most common mistakes, such as buying a very untamed, unmanageable bird or buying an unhealthy bird.

Health Guarantees

Any reputable breeder or pet store will offer some sort of written health guarantee. Generally, these guarantees give you a window of time in which you can take your lovebird to an avian veterinarian for an exam. The exam can often cost more than the bird. However, when

Sample Health Guarantee

Your new bird (band number or other identifying information) is guaranteed healthy and free of disease. You can get confirmation of this by taking your bird to a qualified avian veterinarian within the next _____ days. This would be by: (insert date here). If your bird is found to have an underlying problem by your avian veterinarian, we will take the bird back and refund your money. Although avian certification is not necessary, we do require that the veterinarian be well-qualified to treat and care for birds and have significant experience in avian medicine.

Young birds are susceptible to many diseases, so we ask that you not expose the bird to any other birds for the first six weeks in your home. This is a standard quarantine period for birds. If you expose the bird to other birds during this time, the health guarantee is no longer in effect.

If your bird should die for any reason during the guarantee period, we reserve the right to have our avian veterinarian perform a necropsy and determine the cause of death. We will make arrangements to pick up the bird within 48 hours. If you do not make the bird available to us within 48 hours

the guarantee is voided. This is because a necropsy must be performed within 72 hours for the results to be accurate and meaningful.

The guarantee does not cover death due to any of the following: exposure to aerosolized chemicals, overheated nonstick cookware such as Teflon or Silverstone, new carpeting, scented candles, air fresheners, heated essential oils, pesticides or herbicides, or other chemicals known to be harmful to birds. The guarantee also does not cover death due to ingestion of dangerous foods such as chocolate or avocado; death due to injury such as flying into windows, drowning, or improper supervision with small children; death due to any physical contact with cats, which carry bacteria known to be dangerous to birds, or injury caused by another pet bird or animal in the home; death due to exposure to drafts.

By signing below, I acknowledge that I understand and accept this guarantee.

Signature of Seller
Signature of Buyer
Date of Agreement

you consider the fact that this may be your pet for 15 or more years, it is well worth the initial investment.

If you do not follow the stipulations of the health guarantee, it will not be enforceable. Many guarantees will specifically list events or conditions that will nullify the agreement. Read these stipulations carefully because they will alert you to the most common dangers to birds, the most vulnerable of pets, and will help you avoid tragedy.

Questions to Ask

You should ask the seller of the lovebird a number of essential questions before agreeing to a purchase. If you have done your research, the answers to these questions will help you determine if this is the right source for your new pet.

Questions for a Breeder
• How often do you breed your pairs?
• What hand-feeding techniques do you use?
• Do you handle and socialize your babies?
• What sort of written guarantee do you offer?
• What foods do you wean your birds on?
• Can I call you with questions and concerns after taking the bird home?

Questions for a Pet Store
• What qualities do you expect in the breeders who supply your birds?
• Do you or the breeder wean the bird?
• Have you been handling the bird regularly?
• What foods have you been feeding the bird daily?
• Can I call you with questions and concerns after taking the bird home?

Recognizing Signs of Illness

Buying a bird that looks sick or depressed just because you feel sorry for it is not a good idea. If you truly feel that trying to save such a bird is your mission, then you should feel free to do so. However, you must remember that such birds will need the attention of an avian veterinarian, and you may have to administer medications for some time to bring the bird to a good state of health. In some cases, you may end up with a chronically ill bird or one that has a long-term, debilitating disease, such as psittacine beak and feather disease (PBFD).

Unfortunately, recognizing a sick bird is often difficult. Birds instinctively hide signs of illness as a natural protection against predators. In the wild, many bird species will actually attack and kill a bird that is injured or sick because they instinctively know this bird may attract predators and threaten the safety of the whole flock.

You have to be observant to recognize the more subtle signs of ill health:
• Slightly fluffed appearance (not when the bird is sleepy)
• Discharge from the nares (nasal area)
• Stained vent (soft feces or diarrhea)
• Wheezing sound
• Feather deformities
• Lethargic or uninterested in activity or interaction

A healthy lovebird will appear active and alert, as does this vocalizing masked lovebird.

A healthy lovebird should have bright eyes, full healthy feathering, be active and alert, and be generally clean and well-groomed. If in doubt, trust your instincts. Remember that young lovebirds have muted colors compared with adult lovebirds. A lovebird may take up to a year to achieve the colors of an adult bird fully. With peachfaced lovebirds, you can sometimes determine the general age of the bird by looking at its beak. A very young bird will still have some black on its beak. However, this is not true of all mutations. For example, pied peachfaced lovebirds do not usually have any black on the beak.

Preparing for the New Arrival

Keeping your bird in a communal part of the home where it can see people and interact with them, even from the confines of the cage, is best. A bird kept in a back room by itself will likely be very lonely, craving the attention of its human flock. Prepare an area before you bring the bird home so the transition can be as smooth as possible. When choosing an area, take into consideration such risks as children or other pets knocking over the cage, fumes from cooking, and drafts from windows.

Make your avian veterinarian appointment before you pick up the bird so you can be sure to get it to the veterinarian before the guarantee

Lovebirds are curious, playful creatures and should be given plenty of toys with which to amuse themselves.

period ends. Make sure the guarantee allows time for delayed test results as long as those tests were performed during the initial guarantee period. Many avian veterinarians are extremely busy and may have trouble booking you within a short guarantee period. It is strongly advised that you take the pet store or breeder up on any veterinarian checkup guarantee. If the bird gets sick or dies and you did not take this step, you will have little recourse. The investment in the well-bird checkup is well worth it. As stated earlier, your lovebird is a long-term investment. Losing a precious pet due to inaction can be a very traumatic experience. Chapter 4, "Avian Health," covers the types of tests you might want to order.

If you plan to buy your lovebird at a pet store, it will sell most of the items you need to bring your bird home. Buy the largest cage you can afford, and make sure it has appropriate bar spacing. The bars should not be so wide apart that the bird could push its head between them, possibly trapping and injuring itself. Lovebirds enjoy climbing, so a cage with some horizontal bars is best. Choose a square or rectangular cage, rather than an oval or circular one. Be sure to get a cage with a grating on the bottom that separates the bird from the bottom of the cage. This helps keep the bird from eating old food that has dropped to the floor, a particular problem if fresh foods fall there and sit for a few hours while you are at work or otherwise out for any extended period. Note that lovebirds cannot be left alone for a weekend the way some other types of pets can be. They will often tip over their food and water and be left with nothing until you return. Their fast metabolism makes it impossible for them to go without food or water for even a couple of days. Having a friend or neighbor check on your bird daily is best.

Lovebirds also love to swing and play, so be sure to buy a nice assortment of toys and a swing. Toys with brightly colored beads, bits of chewable wood or leather strips, and bells tend to be their favorites. Be aware that some toys made for birds may actually be dangerous. Avoid copper bells and toys with zinc chains or links as these can cause heavy metal poisoning (see Chapter 4, "Avian Health"). Buy more toys than you need for the cage so you can rotate them occasionally and keep your bird interested in its environment. Toys should also be replaced if they become permanently soiled or damaged in such a way that they could present a hazard to your bird. You should realize that many toys labeled safe for birds may not be safe for *your* bird. Your bird's size and level of destructiveness will determine if some toys should be avoided (see Chapter 5, "Safety Issues"). Also purchase some extra bowls. Most cages come with two or three bowls. A bird should get water, seed, pellets, and some fresh foods each day, so extra bowls will make your life easier. In fact, you should get twice the number of bowls you need. This way, if

you are too busy to wash bowls one morning, you have some extra clean ones ready to put into the cage.

If you are buying directly from a breeder, be sure to purchase the cage and accessories and set them up before you bring the bird home. The breeder may even have a good suggestion about where to find the best cages and toys.

The most important question to ask the seller of the bird is, "What is the bird eating now?" If possible, purchase the same type of seed and pellets so that the bird has an easier transition. You can change these later by slowly adding the new foods to the old ones. However, you do not want to force a bird to make a dietary change while it is already going through the stress of transition to a new home. Many breeders will supply a week's worth of the current seeds and pellets the bird is eating to help with the transition.

When your bird arrives home, put it into its new cage and let it get comfortable with the surroundings. If it begs to be taken out by hanging on the side of the cage or running along the doors, go ahead and handle it for a few minutes at a time. However, you should continue to put the bird back into its cage regularly so it gets used to its new space and starts to eat. In fact, it is a good practice to resist always taking your bird out when it begs for attention. This way, you do not create a situation in the future where the bird squawks persistently if you are busy. Some lovebird owners note that their birds play quite sweetly with them for about half an hour and then seem to get a little nippy or agitated. Lovebirds have a very fast metabolism and can become a bit irritible if they do not get back into the cage to eat and drink water. They generally should be given a break to refresh themselves after about an hour of playing.

Observe your bird's behavior and vitality closely for the first three to four days. Replace the paper daily so you can watch for changes in feces and also see if the bird is really eating. If you have any doubts about whether the bird is eating or not, contact the pet store or breeder immediately to discuss your concerns.

Quarantine Practices

If you have other birds in the house, you should quarantine the new bird until all veterinary test results are back. You should also wait another six to eight weeks for any visual signs of illness in case you get false-negative results when testing for diseases.

The spread of infectious diseases among parrots can be utterly devastating. If you suspect one of your birds is ill, isolate it immediately. Do not purchase any birds if you suspect you already have a problem in your home or aviary. You must first investigate the illness, eliminate any

Lovebirds should be given a variety of perches to keep their feet healthy. Blue and yellow masked lovebirds.

What Is a Quarantine?

To quarantine, you basically totally isolate the new birds from the old birds. You take care to scrub your hands thoroughly after handling the new birds. Deal with the new birds only after you are done taking care of your established birds. When you wash your hands, be sure to scrub with a nail brush so nothing is left under your fingernails. The leading veterinary experts on avian viruses will tell you that virus particles can get under the nails and be spread to other birds. Feather dust, feces, and contaminated foodstuffs can spread disease. Some viruses are extremely stable, such as the pox virus. Everything must be separate for the new and the old birds. Do not mix food or water bowls. Do not mix foodstuffs.

If you inadvertantly expose one of your old flock to the new bird and then see signs of disease in the new bird, you must now also separate from the rest of your flock any of your old birds who were exposed to the suspect bird. This includes birds who were in the same airspace. Airspace is defined as a confined or close-proximity area in which birds may be exposed to feather dust, feces, dried dust of feces, or foodstuffs of sick birds. Airspace is shared even in outdoor aviaries due to breezes or if cages are stacked and feathers can drop down into other cages. Remember, you can carry disease on your shoes as well. Only you can judge the amount of exposure you may have to anything that could be in the air. You know how easily you can catch a cold? Apply this principle to the care of your birds when you add a new member to the household.

sources, and thoroughly sterilize cages and the home before even considering adding a new bird. Many people think that setting these standards is overreacting. Many people will knowingly sell diseased birds. You are the last defense against the spread of disease among your pets or breeder birds.

Many people do not have to consider this issue because the lovebird will be their only pet. In that case, you should still remember these precautions should you visit a bird fair or pet store with birds. If you handle these birds or get feather dust on your clothing, you should shower and change when you arrive home before you handle your own pet. This simple precaution will help you keep your new pet as healthy and free of disease as possible.

Chapter Three
General Care

Diet and Nutrition

Lovebirds require a varied diet made up of a quality small hook-bill seed mix, fresh and cooked vegetables, pellets, and some grains. Some species relish such treats as figs and bits of apple and pear. In fact, Abyssinian lovebirds adore mission figs, which should be a regular part of the diet. If you buy dried fruits, be sure to buy only sulfite-free brands, which are usually available at health-food stores. Fresh fruits are fine, but vegetables are generally more nutritious and should be the emphasized fresh element of the diet. A dried egg food or mashed hard-boiled egg can be given during breeding season. Fresh foods should not be left in the cage more than one or two hours so as to avoid bacterial contamination of the food-stuffs, which can make a bird seriously ill.

All seed mixes are not created equal. You want to be sure to purchase a mix that is fresh; this means that the seeds are not dead and can be germinated and sprouted. A

Brightly colored pellets will often entice even the pickiest eater.

good test is actually to try to sprout your seeds. If they do sprout after three days, this is a quality mix. If not, you will want to try another brand or store. Even a quality brand of seed can have problems if it sits on a pet store shelf for too long. In fact, if you ever open a bag of seed or pellets and find cobweblike strings or detect a musty or moldy odor, do not feed your bird these items. Return the package to the pet store.

Generally, the seeds intended for the smaller hookbills such as love-birds are called one of the following: small hookbill, hookbill junior, or lovebird-conure mix. If none of these are available, a cockatiel mix without sunflower seeds should be fine, but also buy a package of safflower seeds if they are not already included in the mix.

Certain lovebirds can be quite stubborn about changes in the diet. However, persistence is often the key with these birds. A warmed-up mixture of green peas, carrots, and corn will often entice them. You can sprinkle a few seeds on top to make it more familiar to your bird. You may have to try a new food for 10 to 14 days before your bird will actually

Sprouted seeds can be a healthy addition to the diet, but should not be stored for more than three days in the refrigerator due to the risk of bacterial growth.

sample it. Attach a sprig of broccoli to the side of the cage; this attracts lovebirds because it is not just food, it is a food toy. Grapes elicit a similar reaction because they roll around. A lovebird's natural playfulness will lead to a bite of these fresh foods.

Grains also play an important role in your lovebird's diet. Bits of sprouted breads can be an enjoyable treat, as can brown rice and cooked or sprouted quinoa, a nutritious South American grain high in protein and calcium.

Pelleted diets have become popular in recent years. You may have to try a number of these to find one your bird likes. Lovebirds prefer a smaller pellet size and like the fruity varieties. Either cockatiel or parakeet sizes should be fine for your bird.

While some of the companies that manufacture these pellets suggest it be the main source of nutrition, many long-time breeders have found that variety in the diet creates happier and healthier birds. A good proportion of each of the major food groups will ensure that your bird has an interesting, stimulating, and balanced diet. A small bowl of seeds and a separate bowl of pellets can be given daily, along with an extra bowl with fresh foods.

One of the most important elements of your bird's diet is water. Fresh, clean water should be available at all times. Dirty, soiled water is a leading cause of bacterial infections. Sometimes you will have to readjust where you put the water bowl if your bird has decided to hang over that particular part of the cage, resulting in soiled water.

Forbidden Foods

Certain foods present a health hazard to parrots. Any food or drink that contains theobromine should not be given; this includes coffee, tea, colas, hot cocoa, and any type of chocolate. Do not feed avocado because it is toxic to many species. This means no guacamole either. Do not feed junk food. While a french fry once a month will not hurt your bird, if you get in the habit of giving sugar-laden or salty foods to your bird, it could get a taste for them and start to beg. Parrots do not excrete salt the way humans do, so salty foods are unhealthy for them. Sugar can increase the heart rate and cause other health problems over the life of your bird.

Birds should never be given any alcoholic beverages. Unfortunately, some people think intoxicating a pet is amusing. This is extremely dangerous and a form of abuse. If you allow your bird unsupervised play, do not leave open containers with alcohol or any of the other forbidden foods because it may test them out of curiousity. Tall glasses with liquid can be a hazard to birds. If your bird attempts to drink the liquid and falls into the glass, it can become trapped and drown. Of course, any bird outside the cage should be supervised, but you must still eliminate any risks in the environment.

Cuttlebone and Mineral Blocks

Before discussing these items, I must state emphatically that grit should not be given to lovebirds. Grit is intended for birds that cannot break the shell of the seed. Parrots easily break that shell. I personally know an avian veterinarian who necropsied a bird that died unexpectedly. A large impaction of accumulated grit had essentially made it impossible for the bird to digest, assimilate, and eliminate foodstuffs properly. Many pet store workers will still hand you the box of grit to take home. They are basing this on outdated information.

Mineral blocks can be a nice addition to the cage. However, read the ingredients on the label. If it contains grit, choose another. In another case, the veterinarian found large amounts of accumulated grit in a parrot, and the owner was truly baffled because she never fed grit. They found the culprit when they read the label of the mineral blocks she had supplied the bird for years.

Cuttlebone supplies calcium for your pet lovebirds. Birds rarely overindulge in this supplement. It has a slight fishy odor when you first open the package, but this dissipates in a few days. Replace the cuttlebone if it becomes soiled or every two months.

Vitamins and Supplements

If you feed your bird a healthy, balanced diet, you do not need to add vitamins to its food or water. In fact, in cases where a bird eats pellets, adding more vitamins can lead to hypervitaminosis, or an excess of certain nutrients. Adding vitamins to water is always a bad idea because it encourages bacterial growth. Many breeders claim that probiotics are good to give birds after they have undergone antibiotic treatment. Although these products will not harm the bird, they are generally not important. These products are derived from mammals and are not specific for avian flora. Most avian veterinarians will tell you that the only effective probiotic would have to be derived from an avian source, such as chickens.

Herbal Supplements

Most herbal supplements have not been fully studied in humans, let alone birds. If you decide your bird needs some sort of herbal supplement, you do this at your own risk. If you are in a desperate situation with a very sick bird, you may want to try some herbal remedies as a last-ditch effort to save your bird. Be sure to research these items carefully before doing so.

One natural supplement that most parrots relish is fresh wheatgrass. This is grown in pots or large flats. It is high in chlorophyll and a number of vitamins, minerals, and amino acids. You simply trim the grass near the base, being careful not to include the dirt, then give it to the bird. It juices the grass with its beak and leaves the dried husks behind. This is the same type of grass used to make wheatgrass juice at health food stores and juice bars. One cau-

tionary note: If you see any mold growing among the roots, you must wash the cut grass thoroughly with a vegetable wash to remove any possibility of contamination. A particularly nice thing about wheatgrass is that you do not have to worry about it spoiling in the cage. The grass simply dries up, and birds do not seem interested in it once this has happened.

Bathing and Grooming

Many lovebirds will dive into their water bowl and take a bath a few times a week. If your bird is not doing this, you might tempt it by splashing your fingers in the water. I often take a large, low bowl and set

Lovebirds are very attracted to the sound of running water, and this can encourage them to take a bath.

Lovebirds are meticulous groomers who will run each feather through their beaks to clean themselves.

it onto the table on a paper towel, then splash my fingers in it to attract the bird. The bird will start to fluff up its feathers and get excited by the splashing. Generally, it will then dive into the bowl and take a bath.

Another method for bathing is to spritz your bird with room temperature water. Some birds enjoy this right away, but some do not. Most birds will come to like it if you continue to do it on a regular basis. Generally, a spritz every other day is good. Birds that are molting or plucking feathers may need it more often. Once a week it is a good idea for the bird to get a thorough soaking to the skin. Make sure when you do help your bird bathe that you do put it onto on a safe perch. Wet feathers weigh a bird down and make flight difficult or impossible.

You do not want your pet to lose its balance and crash to the floor.

As pet birds have increased in popularity, so has the availability of fun accessories to help you better enjoy your time with your bird. One such accessory is a special shower perch with suction cups that you can attach to the wall of your shower. This allows your bird to have a nice rain shower with you. Make sure the diameter of the perch is appropriate for lovebirds; they need to have a good grip so as not to slip to the floor. Direct the showerhead in such a way that the bird mainly gets a misty shower and not the direct force of the water. Be careful about letting your bird sit high up on the shower rod. A clipped bird that is wet from the rising steam could lose its balance.

That is a long fall, and the bird could be seriously injured, possibly breaking a leg or wing.

Cleanliness

Food bowls, water, cages, and the surrounding environment need to be kept clean. Many birds like to make *bird soup* by dropping food into their water bowl. Sometimes changing the location of the bowl with remedy this, but some birds will carry dehydrated carrots all the way across the cage to the water bowl. Water bottles do not solve the problem of unclean water. Food gets trapped in the tube the first time the bird drinks from it. Frankly, they are actually harder to clean properly. The best way to have fresh water is to have additional clean bowls. You can remove the old bowl and pop the new one in when you are in a hurry and do not have time to clean the water bowl thoroughly. I have three times the number of bowls as necessary just for this reason, and some of my messier birds will need three changes a day when they are feeding young. The hotter the weather the higher the risk that bird soup will turn into a dangerous bacterial stew.

Did you know that dried fecal matter from a parrot with psittacosis who is shedding the virus will present a danger to other birds for up to three or four months? Many people think once the poops have dried up they are not a hazard, but that is not true. You can have an asymptomatic bird who then starts to shed the virus. The dust from the dried poops gets into the air, and suddenly all your birds are infected with psittacosis. Pet birds depend completely on humans to keep their environment safe and as pathogen-free as possible.

Some birds will actually eat their own feces. You must have a cage with a grated bottom that separates your birds from the waste on the bottom of the cage if this is the case. However, this setup does not eliminate all problems. Such birds may also have a gap in their nutrition they are trying to fill. Try increasing the variety in their diet if you notice this behavior.

You can replace the papers on the bottom of the cage daily. However, at least once a week, you should do a thorough cleaning. You might want to get a small carrying cage for your bird so it can sit in there while you do this. This cage can be convenient for veterinarian visits as well. Scrub down all gratings and perches. You can put wood perches in the sun to dry. Remember that wood is a prime material for the buildup of bacteria, so replace wood perches and other wood items every few months or even earlier if they become too soiled to clean. Cage parts can be broken down and soaked in a 30:1 dilution of water to household bleach. All organic matter must be removed from the cage before you soak it in bleach for it to be fully effective.

In general, a clean environment will reduce your bird's risk of bacterial infection. In the wild, birds can poop

A lovebird watches his owner clean his cage.

where they may and fly off. In your home, they are essentially captive to their cage much of the time and in very close proximity to their waste materials and any food that has fallen to the floor. A bird does not know that eating a bit of apple that has been sitting on the floor for three days is a bad idea. So human keepers must make such tidbits unavailable.

Emergency Preparedness

Your pet bird depends on you for its safety and well-being. Therefore, you must be prepared should it need you to act quickly and decisively in the face of an emergency. No one wants to be in the midst of a natural disaster and realize they are not at all prepared. Take the time to put together an emergency plan and supplies for every possible situation. If you do so, you have a good chance of saving your bird in the face of even the gravest situation.

The Home Preparedness List

Be sure to have these supplies on hand for any emergency, whether it be a fire, natural disaster, or bleeding injury. This list is more specifically for pet bird owners. Breeders would have many other items on hand to deal with slow crops, dehydration, and other issues.

• Styptic powder (for toenails, not skin)
• Corn starch and household flour (for bleeding skin/feathers)
• Hemostat
• Needle-nosed pliers

- Tweezers
- Scissors
- Veterinarian tape/self-sticking wrap
- Towels for handling birds
- Carriers for removal of birds
- Emergency water supply
- Emergency food supply
- Survival blankets (these can supply warmth when electricity is not available)
- Heating pad
- Pedialyte
- Betadine
- Distilled water
- Brooder/hospital cage (plastic reptile container will often work for most small-to-medium parrots)
- Emergency phone list

Blood Feather Emergencies

This is an emergency no one wants to think about. Your bird is bleeding profusely and you cannot stop it. If your bird panics, it may bite you. You will need corn starch or household flour to stop the bleeding, a towel for holding the bird, hemostats or needle-nosed pliers, and a good set of tweezers. First try to stop the immediate bleeding with the corn starch or flour. Remember that styptic powder is good only on toenails. It burns on live tissue and will make handling your bird in this possibly life-threatening situation harder.

If you can stop the immediate bleeding emergency, then take the bird to the veterinarian to remove the feather and assure that your bird is fine. Remember that the bleeding can easily start again. The hollow shaft of the feather is like a hose and can cause serious blood loss should the bleeding start again without you realizing it or when you are not home. Substantial blood loss can result in the death of the bird.

If you need to get that feather out now, get a good grip at the base of the broken feather with the pliers or tweezers. Give a good, deliberate pull to remove the feather from the base. Do not twist or hesitate. Quick and clean is best because you do not want to break the feather close to the skin, which can make removal very difficult.

You may need someone to towel the bird and handle it for you while you find the culprit and remove it. A good idea is to have some people you know you can count on in such an emergency. Prepare them in advance for the possibility. If you are having difficulty, do not wait: Take your bird to a veterinarian immediately to have the blood feather properly removed.

Bird Emergency Contact List

This is similar to the list parents put onto the fridge for their baby-sitters. It should list the names and telephone numbers of your veterinarian, a backup veterinarian, poison control, and friends who have agreed to come over and help you should you need help with your bird. Remember, prepare your friends in advance for the job they might have to do so they are not nervous and hesitant when they actually have to help. This will also help you to know who should not be on your list because they will be too uncomfortable or fearful handling your bird. You want someone who is confident about helping.

Some emergencies require even greater preparedness. A household fire could be a time of great panic. While you might not feel at risk for this type of emergency, it is always a possibility. You do not want to be searching for pet carriers and towels should you ever have to get out of your home quickly in the event of a fire.

If you live in an area prone to any major natural events such as hurricanes, tornadoes, or earthquakes, you definitely need to make special preparations to ensure you are prepared to care for your pet after such a disaster. Two general rules of thumb that are particularly important for people who live in areas where disasters such as earthquakes and tornadoes can strike with little warning are:

1. Never let yourself get down to your last bag of seed/pellets.

2. Never let yourself run low on bottled water.

After a natural disaster, getting supplies can be extremely difficult. You do not want to realize you have no tap water and see your pet bird looking up at you with a thirsty look on its face. Obviously, you can make do with other foods in the home. However, if you have a finicky eater, you do not want to be caught only with foods your bird will not touch. Keeping enough seed, pellets,

favorite foods, and water on hand to last five to seven days for all your birds is best.

If you live in an area where you might be asked to evacuate, you may not be able to bring your bird with you if you wait until the last minute. It is best in such a situation to be an *early bird* and evacuate at first warning. This way you can calmly pack up your pet and take it to a location where you know in advance you will be allowed to keep it. If you think every motel will allow your two lovebirds, cockatiel, and Pomeranian, you are wrong. You need to do your research in advance so you know where to go in an evacuation. Public shelters will not allow pets in most cases.

In all these situations, you must have enough carriers for all your birds and other pets. If you have one carrier that is shared among your birds for veterinarian visits or the like, you will not have an easy time evacuating. As most people know, you cannot put birds who do not know each other into such a small, enclosed space. Fighting is bound to ensue.

Small carriers can be bought for a very reasonable price. You can use a standard pet kennel and add your own perch, purchase feed cups that fit in nicely, and make sure it is outfitted properly for your bird. If you have a bird who panics when confronted with a carrier, be sure you keep a towel near the carrier so it is readily available should you need to wrap your bird quickly.

The cage should be big enough to give your bird room to flap its wings.

and chimneys. You not only endanger the life of your bird, but you risk the health and lives of your human family as well.

Remember that in an emergency situation you will not be thinking clearly. You will be concerned about your safety, the safety of your family, and the safety of your pet. This is not the time to figure out where an extra bag of seed is to throw in the car. This is not the time to wonder how you will evacuate your six birds with two carriers. Preparation is the key to coping during natural disasters.

You should have a portable evacuation kit on hand. This should include seeds, pellets, dried fruit and vegetables without sulfites added, bottled water, and your bird's favorite treats. Keep this near your regular emergency kit since you may need this as well should your bird panic and break a blood feather or injure itself during this time of high anxiety. Also include special thermal (camping) blankets to provide warmth should you lose electricity.

Do not ever use any sort of outdoor grill to supply heat in a home after the loss of electricity. These produce deadly carbon monoxide. They are burning fuel. They must be used only outside. Anything that burns produces fumes. This is why stoves and fireplaces have vents

Exercise and Amusement

Birds need exercise just as any other living creature does. If you supply your bird a cage of sufficient size and add a variety of swings and toys, your bird will spend quite a bit of time swinging, climbing, and showing off in its cage. A separate play stand with various perches can also be a good place for your bird to climb and play.

Your bird will be happiest when you and the family are home. Even if you are too busy to take your bird out of the cage, you can make it feel like part of the flock by talking to it and watching its antics. Lovebirds are clownish creatures and love to perform. They will swing from toys and leap from branch to cage wall. They will ring a bell to see if you react. If your bird feels you interact with it during these times, it will be less likely to act out and demand attention, although on occasion most birds will try to get you to take them out of the cage.

Playing with your bird regularly is important. However, do not play with the bird constantly for the first few weeks or months and then, when the novelty wears off, barely handle it. Try to figure out how much time you think you will have for your bird over the long haul, then give your bird periods of focused attention out of the cage.

The remarkable intelligence of parrots requires that they have a varied and stimulating environment. If you put one plain wooden swing and one hanging toy in the cage indefinitely, your bird will become bored. Put as many toys as you can reasonably fit into the cage but still give the bird room to flap its wings. I have one Fischer's lovebird who likes to fly in his cage; he literally hovers in midair, furiously flapping his wings. He also loves my reaction to this and will repeat it over and over if I watch and tell him what a wonderful flyer he is. I would not want to overcrowd his cage with toys and perches because this would make hovering without hitting his wings difficult.

Parrots who are neglected and live alone in a cage can develop a number of behavioral problems. They can become nippy and aggressive. Some will begin to pluck themselves bald, even going so far as to break the skin. Once such a behav-

ior becomes ingrained, it can be very difficult to reverse the problem.

If you consider your pet bird a member of the family and treat it accordingly, you will generally have a well-adjusted, fun pet. Remember that birds are largely confined to their cages between play sessions. Dogs and cats are free to roam about the house and sometimes even have free access to a yard. They are not locked in a cage until the owner decides the bird can come out.

A certain bird shop I have visited keeps birds from the smallest finches to the largest macaws. Many of these intelligent creatures are housed in too-small cages without a single toy. One large cockatoo looked utterly miserable. A friend's daughter, a teenager with a strong bond to animals and birds, could not

Have some special treats to give your bird when out of its cage, such as this slice of apple.

stand to see this. She went over to the toy section and picked up a toy, then put it into the cage. You would have had to have seen the transformation in this bird's mood to understand how clearly it hungered for some type of play and stimulation. We left with smiles on our faces, imagining the store workers scratching their heads, trying to figure out how this bird managed to secure the toy. Certainly, a bird that appears happy and playful will sell better than one sitting miserably on his perch, crouched down and depressed. Giving the bird the five-dollar toy made much more sense to help sell this bird worth well over a thousand dollars.

Birds are not objects to make living rooms more colorful. They are living, thinking, feeling creatures and deserve respect and the best care and attention humans can give them. If you are unable to do this, you should not keep them as pets. Needless to say, I warn people about this store and have come to call it a medieval prison for birds. Do not buy even a bag of seed from any store that treats living creatures this way.

If you do see signs of neglect or abuse in a store, report them to your local humane society immediately.

Time Away from Home

If you are gone for long periods during the day, you might consider leaving the radio or television on for your bird. Keep the volume low so the bird can enjoy the sounds but

An inexpensive hospital brooder can be made with a plastic reptile container, stand-alone perch, and heating pad. Food and water bowls can be placed on the floor.

can also take little naps during the day. Many birds love music with tropical sounds, such as rain forest or mood music. The waterfalls and birds chirping in the background can be very soothing and comforting to a bird alone at home all day. Remember that when you first come home, your bird will want immediate contact. Even a few words and greetings can be a welcome gesture. If you completely ignore your bird for the first hour you are home, you may start to notice the bird squawks for you. The official term for this is a contact call. It is basically the bird touching base with the flock. You have been gone all day, and now the bird wants to confirm that you are with the flock again. In the wild, these contact calls are used to keep track of other members of the group. Some larger species of parrots have contact calls that can reach across miles of dense woodlands or rain forest. Parrot species use their voices for a purpose. If you understand this, you can avoid a situation where vocalizations become excessive or overly disturbing. Many times I have noticed that when one of my birds calls to me from another room, if I just give a quick answer, they quiet down. However, I never reinforce screaming by yelling back at the bird. Chapter 6, "Behavior and Training," discusses problematic noise.

If you have a very long work day and are gone on average more than 12 hours a day, you might consider having a pair of birds rather than a single one. However, you will sometimes have to work a little harder to keep them both tame because they will often become more interested in each other than in the humans who live with them.

Most people find that a lovebird has a short attention span. It can become extremely active, almost agitated, when out with its owner. Short play sessions a few times a day work better than one long, extended play session. This gives the bird time to eat and drink between sessions and helps you avoid the nippiness that can come from an overtired or overexcited bird. It also helps establish the rules of going in and out of the cage. The bird will begin to see that going into the cage is not the end of all play for the day. Even short, five-minute play sessions can do much to improve your bird's behavior and level of contentment. If you have only a minute, do not waste it. Take your bird out for a minute and give it a few strokes around the ear. Although it might want more time with you, if you do this frequently, the bird will come to understand that you plan to handle it again during the day.

Chapter Four
Avian Health

The Avian Veterinarian

An avian veterinarian is not a typical veterinarian. Although all veterinary programs require the study of avian medicine to some degree, most studies are dedicated to the more common domestic pets and agricultural animals. An avian veterinarian has taken special courses and training in avian medicine and probably learned his or her specialty by working with another qualified avian veterinarian. Avian medicine is quite different from mammalian medicine. For example, the lungs of birds dramatically differ from those of mammals. Therefore, specific information about the use of anesthetics is necessary for a veterinarian to administer such medications properly without killing the bird. Even a qualified avian veterinarian will admit this is a difficult task and that even with adequate training and experience, serious problems can still arise.

A young white masked lovebird.

Two types of veterinarians are excellent for birds: those who are avian certified and those who may not have taken certification tests but have vast experience with birds. A good avian veterinarian will keep abreast of the latest developments in avian medicine, attending conferences and training seminars to keep his or her knowledge as current as possible. When you find a top-notch avian veterinarian you will quickly learn from that individual just how much misinformation is out there.

One of the most disconcerting experiences can be when a veterinarian cannot identify the species of bird you bring to him or her. Although hundreds of parrot species exist, anyone with adequate experience with birds will at least be able to recognize the basic family of a pet parrot, such as Amazon, lovebird, or conure. Veterinarians and technicians do not have to expend much effort to learn something about the various species of pet birds. Evidence that they have not taken the time to do so may be reflected in the quality of care they give your bird.

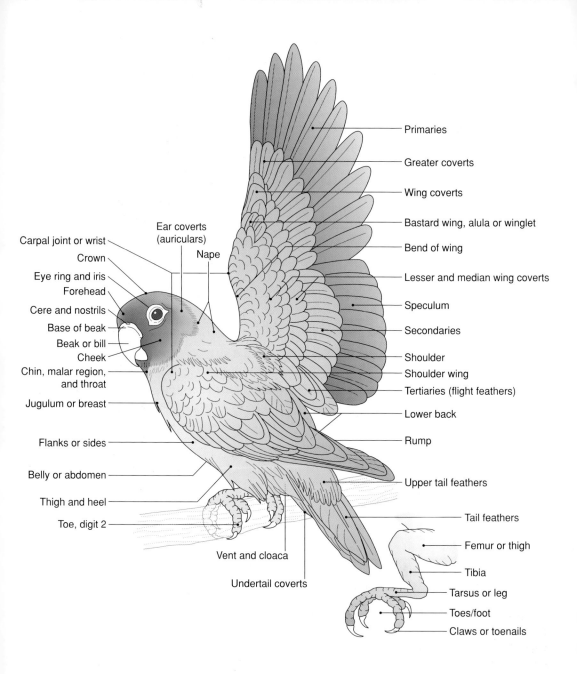

Primaries

Greater coverts

Wing coverts

Bastard wing, alula or winglet

Bend of wing

Lesser and median wing coverts

Speculum

Secondaries

Shoulder

Shoulder wing

Tertiaries (flight feathers)

Lower back

Rump

Upper tail feathers

Tail feathers

Femur or thigh

Tibia

Tarsus or leg

Toes/foot

Claws or toenails

Ear coverts
(auriculars)

Nape

Carpal joint or wrist

Crown

Eye ring and iris

Forehead

Cere and nostrils

Base of beak

Beak or bill

Cheek

Chin, malar region,
and throat

Jugulum or breast

Flanks or sides

Belly or abdomen

Thigh and heel

Toe, digit 2

Vent and cloaca

Undertail coverts

The external anatomy of a lovebird.

Choosing a Veterinarian

The organization for avian veterinarians is called The Association of Avian Veterinarians *(http://www.aav.org)*. This can be a good place to start in your search for a good doctor for your bird. However, you should also try to find someone who can personally recommend a veterinarian. This should be a person who has used this veterinarian's services for some time and has had positive experiences. This is not to say no bird should ever have died under the veterinarian's care. Birds are extremely vulnerable creatures prone to fast-moving ailments to which they can quickly succumb before a veterinarian can intervene. It simply means they have given proper and appropriate care to their feathered patients. A reference from a bird store or breeder can also be valuable. These people tend to visit veterinarians on a much more frequent basis than the typical pet owner and will have a good idea of the quality of care available in their area.

New Bird Exam and Wellness Checkups

Establish a relationship with a qualified avian veterinarian right away. You do not want to wait until your bird is sitting ruffled up on the bottom of the cage to start searching the yellow pages for help. The best way to establish this relationship is by having a new bird exam within a few days of purchasing your pet.

Standard tests are cloacal swab, fecal Gram's stain, and complete blood count. Most of these tests can rule out bacterial or fungal infections, although more extensive testing may be done, such as antigen tests for *Giardia* or DNA probe analysis for psittacine beak and feather disease (PBFD). Discuss the importance of these tests with your avian veterinarian as the costs can run high if you order all of them. In any event, the veterinary exam will cost more than the typical lovebird, and this should not be the only determinant of what tests you have performed.

If you have any members of your household who do not have fully competent immune systems due to very young or old age, organ transplant, or other illnesses, you should definitely test for psittacosis and avian tuberculosis. These are the few infectious diseases that birds can pass on to humans. Psittacosis causes a flulike illness. It is very treatable with antibiotics, both in birds and humans. If you have other birds in the home, checking for PBFD is probably a good idea. This is a devastating, incurable disease, and you do not want to pass it on to the other birds in your home.

Your veterinarian will weigh your bird and record this number. This is an important number to know. If your bird's weight should drop dramatically between veterinarian visits, you will be alerted to a possible serious health problem.

The initial well-bird exam will give you a good idea of the competency and manner of an avian veterinarian. You can then decide if you want to continue care with this particular practitioner. If you feel uncomfortable with a veterinarian, you should seek care elsewhere. You always want to feel that your bird is being handled in a compassionate, expert manner and that your veterinarian is willing to explain what he or she is doing and why. One of the biggest complaints I have heard is when a veterinarian seems annoyed when he or she has to explain the care being given. This can be especially disconcerting if you know quite a bit about birds and want to take an active role in your bird's treatment. A good veterinarian will take the time to explain things to you without impatience or condescension. This is the same treatment you would want from doctors treating you, so you are fully within your rights to expect this from the doctor treating your beloved pet.

Diseases and Vaccinations

A number of diseases are specific to parrots. Some are treatable, some are chronic and devastating. If you understand these diseases, you can take measures to avoid them from the beginning. This is especially important if you have an established pet bird and want to add another to the family. All avian diseases cannot possibly be listed here, so this section will focus on the most common ones. You can dramatically reduce your bird's risk of acquiring these diseases by following the basic rules of hygiene and quarantine and by being circumspect about the source of your pet bird.

Viral and Related Diseases

Viruses are everywhere. Many viruses are extremely stable in the environment and do not need a living host to survive. For this reason, they can persist for many months in your home or aviary, just waiting for a new victim. Total disinfection of the home or aviary is necessary should any of these viruses be detected in your pet bird. Virus particles can be carried on your clothing, hair, and under your fingernails. If you come into contact with an infected bird at a bird show or store, you can take the virus home to your pet. Read thoroughly the section about prevention later in this chapter so that you can avoid inadvertently infecting your pet bird.

Not all species are equally susceptible to every virus. A species must have a receptor on its cells to which the virus can attach. This means the opposite is true as well: you must protect certain species more diligently against certain viruses. Another issue of grave concern is the ability for certain birds to serve as asymptomatic carriers of a disease. A seemingly healthy, uninfected bird can spread the disease through an aviary, the owner never suspecting who the actual source is.

Some birds will be exposed to a virus and be able to mount a sufficient immune response to destroy it. These birds can either become immune and no longer pose a threat to other birds or they can become silent carriers, putting other birds at risk of infection.

To diagnose infection, a veterinarian will perform specific tests. Some tests are more accurate than others. In the case of certain diseases, the veterinarian will recommend retesting at a later date. Follow your veterinarian's instructions closely to give your bird the best chance of survival.

In the case of some viruses, the bird will rapidly deteriorate and die. Unfortunately, in these cases, diagnosis is made during the postmortem exam. Whenever a bird dies unexpectedly and suddenly, you must have a necropsy performed by an avian veterinarian. The veterinarian will send samples to the lab for pathological examination. You want to rule out an infectious disease that could still be present in the home environment. If such a disease is present, you must thoroughly disinfect your home before even considering the purchase of another pet bird.

Young birds tend to be the most susceptible to these diseases. This is because their immune system has not fully developed. However, some viruses can take years to kill a bird, causing slow destruction of the infected cells and organs.

Often the first indications of an underlying viral disease are recurrent bacterial and fungal infections. For example, stubborn infestation by mites in budgerigars is often a secondary sign of an underlying immunodeficiency or disease. A virus undermines a bird's immune system, making it vulnerable to secondary bacterial and fungal infections, particularly opportunistic pathogens. A human parallel to this is human immunodeficiency virus (HIV). Patients do not succumb to HIV; they succumb to secondary infections because their bodies can no longer mount a sufficient immune response to bacteria, fungi, and viruses. A healthy immune system enables people and birds to fight off many infectious agents.

Psittacine beak and feather disease (PBFD). The mere mention of this viral disease strikes fear into the hearts of breeders and pet bird owners. It is a circovirus, and Old World parrots (Africa, Australasia) are most susceptible. Fatality can occur in a few months or a year, or a bird can be chronically infected for more than a decade. The proper adherence to rules of quarantine and protection of your birds from exposure will dramatically reduce your risk of bringing this devastating disease home (see the following section about prevention).

PBFD is thought to be endemic in wild cockatoos in Australia. Lovebirds, along with cockatoos, African grey parrots, and eclectus parrots are the most vulnerable to this virus. Young birds are the most susceptible to infection. The most obvious signs of PBFD are feather deformities. Feathers may appear twisted, broken, bent, or otherwise deformed. In neonates, death can occur rapidly; progression of the disease causes diarrhea, lethargy, and sudden weight loss. Death can be so rapid in these young birds that you may never see the signs of feather deformity.

In chronically infected birds, signs often become most obvious during molts. New feathers will not lose their sheaths or may break off. Some feathers may appear curled in upon themselves or not fully developed. Changes to the beak are also sometimes evident.[2]

PBFD spreads fast and efficiently. The viral particles that cause this disease are very stable in the environment. A person can go to a bird show where infected feather dust settles onto their clothing. They then go home and handle their pet without first showering and changing clothes, possibly infecting their pet.

This virus can also penetrate the egg's shell or can be passed from parents to the chick. It can be spread by dried, airborne fecal matter and by feather dust particles.

A DNA probe analysis can be done to test for the virus in a bird's blood. The bird should be retested in

90 days per your veterinarian's instructions. Some birds will test negative at the second test, which may indicate the bird has successfully destroyed the virus. A test can also be done on fecal matter and feathers found in the home or aviary to determine if it is still present in the environment, presenting a risk to other birds should they be introduced to the home.

Any bird testing positive for PBFD should be immediately isolated from all other birds. The area where the bird was housed must be thoroughly disinfected. Any birds exposed to this bird or housed in the same general air space, even if they were housed outdoors, must be tested for the virus. Never expose other people's birds to your PBFD-positive bird. Remember that you essentially carry your bird with you wherever you go if you handle it and then wear the same clothes out of the house. Do not handle your infected bird then go to a pet store and handle their birds.

Some chronically infected birds can live a relatively normal life, but they must be protected from secondary infection through meticulous disinfection of their living space and food and water bowls. They should be in as stress-free an environment as possible and be fed a well-balanced, healthy diet.

Polyoma virus. Neonatal and young lovebirds are vulnerable to infection with the polyoma virus. For this reason, birds under a year of age should be vigorously protected from

[2]Ritchie, Branson. *Avian Viruses: Function and Control.* Lake Worth, FL: Wingers Publishing, Inc., 1995.

exposure. Your avian veterinarian can test for polyoma virus. He or she may recommend a polyoma virus vaccination. This is one of the few vaccinations widely available for parrots. Although the vaccination has been surrounded with some controversy, if you breed lovebirds and therefore will have young birds around, you may want to consider vaccinating your young. This is especially true if you do not have a closed aviary and plan to add new birds to your flock. Discuss the pros and cons with your trusted veterinarian.

Progression of polyoma virus infection in neonates can be rapid. Sometimes the first indication that the virus is present in an aviary is when a breeder has multiple sudden deaths of newborn birds. One of the indications of this disease in neonates is a darkening of the abdomen, which is due to internal bleeding that can be seen through their thin skin. Some young birds will fight the virus only to succumb during the stress of weaning. Signs include diarrhea, weight loss, incessant crying as if hungry, and the inability to maintain a normal body temperature. Any aviary that sees these signs should immediately stop breeding their birds until the situation can be properly handled. No birds should be sold, and no new birds should be brought into the home. No known cure exists for polyoma.

Polyoma is a very stable virus and can survive many attempts to eliminate it through the use of disinfec-

tants. Be sure to follow the suggestions later on in this chapter to make sure you properly disinfect a home or aviary in which this virus has been detected.

Pacheco's disease. Pacheco's is a herpesvirus. All psittacines are susceptible to this virus, but Old World parrots do seem to be more resistant. Conures can be carriers of Pacheco's. Infected susceptible birds can die suddenly or develop anorexia, diarrhea, and tremors.

Proventricular dilatation disorder (PDD). Another heartbreaking viral disease, it is often called macaw wasting disease. It has been seen in many other psittacine species as well. It is a chronic disease with an extended incubation period. Signs can be lethargy, going light or anorexia, regurgitation, and undigested seeds seen in fecal matter. No cure exists as of this writing.

Bacterial Diseases

A variety of bacterial organisms can make your pet bird sick. These can be spread by other birds or they can colonize in cages or aviaries where fecal matter and rotting foodstuffs are allowed to sit.

Psittacosis. During the 1940s, a large number of budgerigars were imported to the United States for one holiday season. They were growing in popularity, and the demand exceeded the supply in the country. Very soon after this large importation, an outbreak of psittacosis occurred in humans. For a while, this resulted in banding laws for budgerigars. These bands allowed health departments to investigate possible outbreaks of the disease better. Most states no longer have such laws. The issue of psittacosis has not gone away, although no epidemics similar to the one in the 1940s have occurred. The most important thing to know about this disease is the fact that it is zoonotic, transmissable from birds to humans.

Chlamydia psittaci is the cause of psittacosis. In birds, signs can be wheezing, sneezing, discharge from the nares, or watery eyes. A fecal stain will show if the bird is actively shedding *C. psittaci*. However, a negative result does not mean the bird is not infected, just that he is not actively shedding infected particles at that moment. Having a blood test for antibodies to *C. psittaci* is best. A positive result will indicate that the bird has been exposed to this bacterium and has mounted an immune response. This could mean one of two things: the bird is now immune and no longer will shed the virus or the bird still carries the virus and can begin to shed it again actively in the future. Many veterinarians will tell you that truly knowing if a bird is free of this pathogen after treatment is not possible. A bird can have a subclinical infection that is not detectable with current tests.

If you have very young children, eldery adults, or any immunosuppressed individuals living in your home or planning to visit, you should test for psittacosis. In healthy adults, psittacosis causes a flulike illness. However, anyone without a fully developed or fully healthy immune system can have more severe, life-threatening symptoms. Psittacosis is a reportable disease, meaning the doctor must notify state health agencies and the Centers for Disease Control when it is detected in humans. You do not hear about cases of this disease very often. Current bird owners do not need to be alarmed if their birds have never shown signs of illness and no family members have had unexplained, extended illnesses. However, anyone who has had a long-term respiratory illness that has not responded to treatment should let their doctor know if they own parrots because the medication for psittacosis is very specific.

You should note that active organisms can remain in dried fecal matter for many months. Therefore, you should throw out any items that cannot be properly disinfected, such as wood perches and toys, if *C. psittaci* is detected in your bird. This bacterial infection can be treated with antibiotics either via medicated seed or through injections. Humans who have contracted the infection are also treated with antibiotics.

Megabacteriosis. Although the name suggests this is a bacterial infection, some veterinary researchers suggest it is not your typical bacteria and even has some characteristics similar to *Candida*. Megabacteria have been of particular concern recently. They are thought to be an opportunistic pathogen. In other words, they may be endemic in the environment, but only birds with underlying immune problems are susceptible to colonization. Some birds may be asymptomatic carriers. Budgerigars, lovebirds, cockatiels, canaries, and finches are susceptible. Problems have been increasing among exhibition budgerigars in the United Kingdom. It is often a wasting disease affecting young birds; these birds lose weight and die. Unfortunately, it is usually diagnosed postmortem by fecal stain or by smears from the liver or spleen.

Sometimes birds infected with megabacteriosis will show blood in the feces. Other signs can be lethargy, grinding of the seed with the beak but not actually ingesting it, unhulled seeds in the feces or being regurgitated, and brownish stains in the feathers around the beak, which is actually blood.

Diagnosis and treatment can be challenging. Culture of the organisms is difficult. The best test seems to be a fecal stain. The most successful treatments have been of birds that were diagnosed within a few days of signs appearing. The main treatment has been with amphotericin B, which is normally used as an antifungal agent in immunocompromised human patients. It must be given twice daily by mouth for 10 to 14 days, which is a rigorous therapy for both the bird and its owner. The treatment is not always effective. Megabacteriosis is an example of a disease that is best prevented with proper sanitary practices, quarantine, and closed aviaries.

Fungal Diseases

Many fungal organisms are opportunistic. This means they essentially prey upon vulnerable hosts. A vulnerable host might be a bird with an underlying viral disease or a bird forced to live in dirty or moldy conditions.

Aspergillosis. *Aspergillus* species generally affect birds who have an underlying immune dysfunction or who have been living in dirty cage conditions. *Aspergillus* species have also been found in unshelled peanuts, so these are not recommended for parrots. Corncob bedding has also been identified as a breeding ground for this fungus, so it is best avoided.

Aspergillus grows in the air sacs of the lungs, causing severe respiratory distress. Most veterinarians will tell you it is a singularly frustrating disease to treat, requiring long-term therapy that often fails. In many cases, the air sacs have been too compromised by the time the disease is recognized. Some other factors that can put birds at risk of infection are immunosuppression due to other underlying factors, too much vitamin A in the diet, the overuse and abuse of antibiotics, and poorly ventilated aviaries.

Candida albicans. This fungal infection is most often seen in young birds being hand-fed. *Candida* can grow in the crop, causing sour or slow crop, or it can grow in the lungs if food is aspirated. The most susceptible adult birds are those living in dirty conditions and those in which antibiotics have been overused and abused. Signs can be regurgitation and slow crop.

Food-Borne and Other Bacterial Infections

Parrots can get food poisoning just as humans can. You should use the same precautions in preparing their food as you would when preparing food for human guests. Do not cut up their vegetables on a cutting board where you recently cut raw chicken or other meats. One of the best disinfectants is Oxygene, which has stabilized chlorine dioxide. One of the reasons I particularly like it is that it is not toxic to humans or birds if any residue remains. Use a fruit and vegetable wash for fresh foods. It not only removes pesticide residues but can help remove any bacteria. Now this does not mean you should take out some smelly sprouted seeds and beans and use the special wash to make them "clean." Rotten food should be tossed. If you have any suspicion that a food has spoiled, trust your instincts and toss it.

Any of the bacteria that contaminate foods and cause illness in humans can cause illness in parrots. Remember, vegetables and fruits can harbor *Escherichia coli* bacteria on the outer skin. You must wash canteloupe and other fruits thoroughly before cutting into them. You can never know for sure if a neighboring farm's cattle waste washed into the fields where they grew the fruits and vegetables you just pulled from your fridge. Some of these bacteria are lethal enough to kill your bird.

The most common problems documented in parrots are the Enterobacteriaceae. For instance, salmonellosis is most commonly due to *Salmonella typhimurium,* and colibacillosis is due to *Escherichia coli.* Human carriers of *S. typhimurium* can infect companion birds, although I am loathe to consider the kind of personal hygiene such people practice.

Other pathogens are *Bordetella avium* in contaminated water, and *Klebsiella pneumoniae* and *K. oxytoca,* which are resistant to many disinfectants and can be transmitted to humans. Wash your hands thoroughly and use a nail brush to make sure no bacteria or other contaminants are lodged under your nails before you prepare your bird's food. In fact, hand washing is by the far the greatest preventive measure for the spread of bacteria and should be done both before and after handling your pet bird or its foods.

Prevention of Diseases

The most important method of prevention is to keep the environment clean. Cages, toys, swings, perches, and food and water bowls should be washed and disinfected regularly. If your bird poops into its water, try moving the bowl to a different location to eliminate the problem. A weekly thorough disinfection of the cage is an excellent policy.

Disinfection Techniques

Before actually disinfecting bowls and cages, you must first remove all traces of organic materials. Organic matter tends to dilute or eliminate the bactericidal and virucidal effects of most disinfectants. Once the items have been scrubbed clean, you can then move on to the disinfection process.

Household bleach is one of the best and least expensive disinfectants. You need add only one part bleach to every 30 parts water to achieve sufficient disinfection. Most people use far too much bleach and are overwhelmed by the smell. Also, use bleach in a well-ventilated area, even at this dilution.

Some commercial disinfectants are specifically formulated for use in aviaries, such as chlorhexidine gluconates and glutaraldehydes. However, be sure you read the instructions carefully. Many of these chemicals require a minimum soaking time and are not effective if the instructions are not carefully followed. Some household disinfectants may be too strong in odor to use around your birds. Generally, putting your bird into a carrier cage then cleaning its main cage in a well-ventilated area is best. Some people will use rubbing alcohol to disinfect smaller items or utensils. However, remember that this requires about 20 minutes of contact time to kill all viruses and bacteria.

Exposure to Outside Birds

I have often seen proud pet bird owners march through a crowded bird mart with their beloved parrot on their shoulder. Nothing could be more risky than this behavior. These marts are crowded not only with birds from multiple sources but many unweaned baby birds, an unfortunate development in the commercial bird world. If any place puts your bird at risk for contracting an infectious disease, this is the place. In fact, if you visit these marts even without your birds, you should follow some very strict guidelines upon returning home. First, leave your shoes outside. After entering the home, immediately toss your clothes into the laundry and wash them in a detergent that contains a bactericidal agent. Some companies now make powder laundry detergents that will kill 99 percent of bacteria if used at the proper temperature. After doing this, go straight to the shower and thoroughly wash your hair and clean under your fingernails. Do not handle your bird until you have done this.

If you purchase items at pet stores or marts where birds are not separate from the products, wash the outer packaging of the item or the item itself before giving it to your bird. This means even washing the plastic seed bags. Although this might seem excessive, I have heard a number of stories of people who had a bird suddenly become ill with a devastating disease after the owner had visited a show or store .

Heavy Metal Toxicity

One of the biggest culprits for heavy metal toxicity is a poorly made cage. Improper manufacturing processes or the use of powder coating that contains lead can create a dangerous environment for a parrot. Parrots love to chew, or even mouth, items. Often the first signs of lead or zinc poisoning, the two most likely metals in a bird's environment, are loss of balance and/or seizures. Some people have described strange head movements in their birds before the veterinarian diagnosed this type of poisoning, a sign of neurological damage. Avoid copper bells, penguin toys with leaded bases, and zinc quick links. Stainless steel links and chains should be used for all toys. If your bird is ever diagnosed with heavy metal toxicity, the treatment can be difficult. The most important thing is to eliminate the source of poisoning in the environment. Otherwise, the bird will

Sources of Zinc and Lead
- Lead curtain weights
- Batteries
- Fishing accessories
- Galvanized wire
- Costume jewelry
- Stained glass leading
- Linoleum
- Toy hangers
- Twist ties
- Galvanized metal dishes

continue to ingest or chew the item that made it sick in the first place. If you suspect heavy metal poisoning, take your bird to the veterinarian immediately.

Recognizing Signs of Illness

In the wild, birds have a primary concern: to protect themselves from predators. A sick or injured bird is a prime target for predators. Because of this, birds have learned to disguise their illnesses. By the time birds show obvious signs of illness, they are very ill indeed. Learning how to recognize the signs of an illness before it progresses to serious disease or death is important.

Too often one hears about birds who have died unexpectedly. The owners lament that they had no idea the bird was sick. However, when questioned about specific signs, most will admit they did see certain changes, but they did not realize these indicated a life-threatening illness. Having a strong sense of certain baseline behaviors is a good idea so you will quickly notice if your bird is acting differently. Look closely at your bird's daily fecal matter so you will be able to recognize when the color and consistency have changed. Here are some specific changes to look for in your pet:

Changes in behavior. A normally independent bird might seem more needy or a normally cuddly bird

These white-faced slate (dark blue) and violet peachfaced lovebirds sit high on the perch, signs of a healthy bird.

might seem standoffish. If a usually playful parrot seems to have lost interest in its toys, this could also be a warning sign. Changes in vocalization, such as a normally talkative bird no longer speaking, can be important signs.

Changes in fecal matter. If feces suddenly become black, more watery, or have changed color in a way that cannot be explained by an unusual addition to the bird's diet, this can be a sign of illness. Remember, diet can greatly affect the color of fecal matter. Therefore, you should know what *your* bird's poops look like when it is healthy rather than compare them to some generalized standard. For example, a bird who eats a brightly colored

pellet as part of the diet might have bright red or purple in its feces, which is simply a result of the dyes in the food. Save the daily droppings the day you are going to the veterinarian to help him or her evaluate your bird's health.

Changes in appearance. A sick bird will often be puffed up more than usual. A very sick bird will appear listless, lethargic, or let its feathers droop. Its eyes will have a tired appearance. The tail may bob as if the bird is breathing more heavily. Signs this extreme require immediate intervention by an avian veterinarian. Again, observe your bird during times of health so you will be more aware of subtle visual changes in appearance.

Other physical changes. Other signs to be on the alert for are discharge around the nares (nose area) or ears; messy vent, indicating diarrhea; and sneezing or a wheezing sound when breathing. Other signs include labored breathing, which is a very serious sign and should never be ignored, and regurgitating food when not associated with mating behavior, particularly if the food seems to be undigested.

Changes in activity. If your bird is sleeping longer and does not seem to be as active or playful, these can be signs of illness. If your bird is sitting puffed up on the bottom of its cage, things have progressed to a very serious stage and you may have only a few hours to get veterinary intervention.

Bleeding. Be prepared for bleeding-type emergencies. Some products on the market will stop bleeding. Styptic powder is good for toenail bleeding. It is painful on open wounds, however, and can cause a bird to mutilate itself. Common household flour can also stop most bleeding. Birds are small creatures and can bleed to death quite quickly. Any bird that has bled significantly should be seen by a veterinarian, even if you have stopped the bleeding.

Cats. If a cat has contact with your bird, even without seemingly breaking the skin, you should take that bird to a veterinarian immediately. Cats have *Pasteurella* bacteria as part of their normal flora. *This bacteria is extremely deadly to birds.*

If your bird has been batted around by a cat, take it to a veterinarian, even if it seems unharmed.

If your pet bird shows any of the symptoms described above, you must take it to a qualified avian veterinarian as soon as possible. Since these signs generally become obvious only after a bird has been sick for quite some time, even a day's delay can mean the difference between life and death. If you have even the slightest doubt that the bird is perfectly fine, trust your instincts and get your pet to a veterinarian as soon as possible.

Making a Hospital Brooder

A good item to have on hand in case your bird starts to show signs of illness is a makeshift hospital carrier (see photo, page 36). You can purchase a plastic reptile container for this purpose. These are inexpensive and come with brightly colored tops with small slits for air. Also purchase a small stand-alone perch and a heating pad. You can place a bird into this brooder and set it onto a heating pad to help your bird retain body heat. Maintaining body temperature is essential. Put a towel between the carrier and the heating pad to transmit the heat more evenly. I prefer to put the heating pad under only one side of the container so the bird can move away from the heat if it prefers. Be sure that you check the bird every five minutes at first until you are sure the temperature has stabilized. If the bird is panting, the pad is too hot. You can either put thicker towels between the brooder and the heating pad or lower the temperature.

Place a few layers of plain paper towels onto the floor of the brooder. Place small, heavy bowls in the bottom of the brooder with water and your bird's food. Do not put fresh food into here because the added heat may encourage bacterial growth. Small glass custard dishes work well for this purpose.

Broken Bones

Should your birds crash into a wall, break a wing, or break a leg, you will need immediate veterinarian

White and blue masked lovebirds.

care. Put your bird into the makeshift brooder because it will be more comfortable there and less likely to fall again and reinjure itself. Never let a frightened bird have free flight in your house. A crash into a wall can break the bird's neck or cause hemorrhaging in the brain. Broken legs can be a challenge to treat because most parrots will spend the majority of their day trying to remove the cast. Expect to revisit the veterinarian a few times while the leg heals. You should never ignore a possibly broken bone because it could set improperly and have a permanent, crippling effect on your bird.

Birds and Antibiotics

Why a special section about antibiotics? Because these are some of the most misunderstood and misused medications on the planet. Overuse of these types of medications in your pet birds can make them vulnerable to fungal infections. Misuse can lead to the development of resistant strains of bacteria, untreatable by your veterinarian.

Many people fear antibiotics. They believe they are inherently bad for humans and for their birds. This belief is unfortunately based on the misuse and abuse of antibiotics and has nothing to do with their true value. Antibiotics are allies when used properly but can create havoc when used improperly.

A green pied peachfaced lovebird.

Antibiotics are bacteriostatic and bactericidal medications. They basically inhibit the growth of or kill bacteria. However, not all antibiotics can destroy all types of bacteria. Over the succeeding generations since the invention of penicillin, many new classes of antibiotics have been created to deal with various bacteria, such as fluoroquinolones, one of the more popular classes used by avian veterinarians (Baytril is an example). If you give the wrong antibiotic for a specific bacteria, you either do nothing or, in some cases, allow the development of more resistant strains.

Antibiotics must be given for a prescribed period of time. Doctors and veterinarians do not prescribe antibiotics for ten days because it sounds like a good amount of time. They do this because they have data to support this time frame to kill an invading pathogen adequately. Therefore, when people do not comply with the proper course just because they see the bird is feeling better, they risk leaving the more resistant bacteria behind. This can result in an even more virulent infection soon after. The bacteria can even mutate and develop resistance to the antibiotic. Then doctors have to take out the bigger guns. Sometimes these stronger antibiotics work, sometimes they do not. Therefore, not following the prescribed course can be life threatening.

Many people do not understand how resistance works. They think a single person becomes resistant to the antibiotic. In fact, the bacteria become resistant. You have, in effect, created a more deadly strain. You might say you have unleashed a bigger, more deadly pathogen on your community as a whole. What this means is that people are responsible for all humans and animals when using antibiotics. Irresponsible use affects everyone.

Many times, a bird will show early signs of infection. These might be a change in fecal consistency, loss of appetite, increased need for attention, increased sleeping, or other, more subtle signs. By the time your bird is sitting on the bottom of the cage, you are in a dire situation. It needs immediate care. The next step is to get the bird to an avian veterinarian within a few hours. The veterinarian will often prescribe an antibiotic based on a smear that he or she looks at under a microscope. The veterinarian should also take a blood sample to send to the lab for further analysis. While waiting for the results to come back would be ideal, if a bird is deathly ill, starting it on something right away while awaiting results is best, even if a specific pathogen has not yet been identified. However, do not rely on this as the only treatment for your bird. Those culture results are important. They will allow your veterinarian to choose the best antibiotic based on antibiotic sensitivity testing.

If the results show the antibiotic you have been giving is not the best choice, discuss with your veterinarian the options for switching over to a more appropriate medication. You do not just want to decide to stop the old and bring in the new. You may have to finish one course before starting the next. Discuss issues such as resistance with your veterinarian. This is important for the long-term health of your bird.

Over-the-Counter Medications

The worst thing you can do for your bird is self-diagnose its illness and then buy antibiotics at the pet store. These are typically mixed in water. They are very broad spectrum and are in almost all cases a complete waste of your money. You should never try to diagnose and treat your bird on your own. At best, these medications give a false sense of security and can cause you to waste valuable time when your bird could be getting proper medical care.

How to Administer Antibiotics

I am a firm believer that medications should be given directly to the bird by syringe in the mouth or injected. Mixing antibiotics in water is a hit-or-miss scenario. How much is it drinking? Is it drinking less because it does not like the taste? Is the bird drinking more because it is thirsty and therefore getting too much medication? The only way to determine if your bird is truly getting the exact, correct dosage is to give it orally. While this can be a struggle with some birds, it is worth the effort. Young human children often do not want to take their medicine, but, as adults, we would never think twice about not making them take it. Your veterinarian can teach you how to restrain your bird properly to administer the medication.

Everything but the Kitchen Sink

Home remedies are all well and good for humans, but do not experiment on your birds. Birds are not mammals. What works on humans does not necessarily work for them. Not giving your bird home remedies during antibiotic therapy is especially important. Some foods can inhibit the efficacy of these drugs. For example, do not add grapefruit seed extract to your bird's water as an extra medication when you are giving it antibiotics. Grapefruit is one of the foods that is well-known by doctors to interfere with the absorption of some antibiotics. Natural is not by definition safe.

Feather Picking

Some people might want to debate whether this topic should go under avian health or under behavior. Because first ruling out bacterial or fungal causes for feather plucking or mutilation is important, I chose the former. Feather plucking can start innocently enough, a few missing feathers on the breast or crests of the wings. However, if you do not take immediate action it can quickly turn into a serious and intractable problem. First, this is being discussed in terms of pet birds. Mating pairs present a different issue because a hen will often clear what is called a brood spot on her belly or will pluck the feathers from her mate's head as part of the breeding process.

Some people believe feather picking is ultimately an issue of hormones. A frustrated bird begins to pick at itself as hormones rage and it has no outlet for these energies. Other veterinarians have named this condition in lovebirds *lovebird pyoderma*. They will first rule out a skin infection and treat for any bacteria or fungus that might be detected. However, the behavior will often continue. Two avian veterinarians in Seattle, Washington, Drs. Donna Kelleher and Tracy Bennett, report success in treating this condition in lovebirds with the use of medication for any identified infection and then the use of an herbal remedy to help the bird who continues to pluck in a manner that can best be described as compulsive behavior.

My best advice is to nip this behavior in the bud as soon as it starts. Do not wait until your bird is partially bald. The faster you deal with it, the more likely it will not become an ingrained, compulsive behavior. In cases where this seems to be more a behavioral than a medical problem, causes have been given such as boredom, frustration, and anxiety. Examine your bird's environment carefully to see what may have triggered the behavior. In one case, an African grey parrot began picking and the owners traced the start of the behavior to the day when they hung a new, large painting on the wall facing the bird's cage. Who knows why this particular painting caused anxiety or stress in this bird, but removal of the painting did solve the problem.

Other sources of anxiety could be a new baby in the home, new pets such as dogs and cats, a new bird that is placed too close to your established bird's territory, or sudden changes in the decor of the home. This is not to say you cannot move your furniture once you own a bird. One of the most effective ways to help a bird remain flexible and amenable to change is to expose it to change on a regular basis early in its life. This can be done by moving its cage, rearranging the inside of the cage, allowing friends to handle the bird, and generally exposing it to new foods and toys on a regular basis. As your bird comes to realize that you will not expose it to anything dangerous, it will be less likely to overreact to changes in its environment. Birds can easily become creatures of habit. So by changing your schedule and routines on a regular basis, you prepare your bird for changes in all aspects of its environment.

A blue pied peachfaced lovebird.

A special note on lovebirds who pick themselves until they bleed: Never use styptic powder to stop skin bleeding. It burns and will cause the bird to become even more aggressive with the wound. Also remember that if the bird ever does create a wound, it should be examined and treated by an avian veterinarian. A solution of Betadine diluted 50 percent with water will protect the wound from infection, and the veterinarian may also recommend a course of antibiotics if any infection is detected. An Elizabethan collar might be necessary to keep the bird from reaching the wound and causing further damage.

Chapter Five

Safety Issues

The Most Vulnerable of Pets

Lovebirds make wonderful, enchanting pets, but they also require special care and a very safe environment in order to live long, healthy lives. In fact, the greatest issue facing pet bird owners is safety. Birds tend to be very delicate pets and are vulnerable to many environmental factors. The fact that many pet birds are not fully flighted means they depend on humans for their physical safety. They must be supervised at all times when outside their cages because they are often the victims of accidents, such as being stepped on or sat on. The natural curiosity of lovebirds can get them into trouble quickly. They may nibble on poisonous plants or get their beaks around something that could shatter. If a bird swallows anything made of glass, this can severely damage its digestive system.

Birds are also very vulnerable to environmental factors such as drafts. Their lungs are extremely sensitive to fumes, so they cannot

A yellow Fischer's split ino.

be exposed to chemicals, smoke, or other airborne toxins. Anyone who is considering bringing a bird into his or her home must understand the various issues that can necessitate some basic changes in how you do things in that home. These pets often require more intensive care and protection than the larger and more common domestic pets—cats and dogs.

Wing Clipping

Although often a topic of controversy, wing clipping must first be distinguished from pinioning. Pinioning is a permanent crippling of a bird's ability to fly. This is often done to geese and other large fowl to regulate their movement yet allow them to remain outdoors. Wing clipping is a completely temporary measure that inhibits a bird's ability to get lift when flying. It should never cause any bleeding and it does not cause pain, although a bird might not like its wing being stretched out during the few seconds necessary to trim the feathers. The first five to seven flight feathers are trimmed to the

A fully flighted bird is a lovely sight, but most homes are not set up in a way to protect such pets from escape.

level just below the coverts. A proper wing trim will allow a bird to fly safely and smoothly to the floor or from one place to another at the same level. However, it does not allow the bird to fly up, thereby preventing accidental escapes into the great outdoors.

Finding the right number of feathers to trim for your particular bird is important. Some birds can get lift if only five feathers are trimmed; for some birds, this will be an adequate trimming. You do not want to overtrim the flight feathers because this will result in the bird not having enough lift to make a soft landing. If after a wing clip your bird drops to the floor like a stone, you have overdone it. Therefore, trimming only five feathers at first and then testing your bird's ability to get lift is a good idea. If the bird is still able to rise when flying or gains too much distance with a single flight, you can trim one or two more feathers. Bird owners should have a professional trim their bird's wings the first few times. You should not try to do this yourself until you have been given a proper demonstration. You must always be on the alert for flight feathers with blood in the shaft. These are called blood feathers. Cutting these can result in dangerous levels of bleeding. If you are not sure you can recognize a blood feather, have a professional do your bird's wing trimming.

Clipping Versus Not Clipping

This issue creates heated debate. Advocates of both sides can be equally vehement about their point of view. The decision whether or not to clip your bird's wings is a completely individual one and should be based on your home environment and the level of safety you can provide your bird. However, I have found that most homes cannot sufficiently protect a fully flighted pet bird from escape.

Most birds are kept in a communal part of the home. This is often the living room or family room. These rooms tend to have doors that lead directly to the outdoors. A fully flighted bird that is allowed to be outside the cage on regular occasions would be at great risk for escape in such a room. All it takes is one ring of the doorbell, a moment where you forget the bird is on your shoulder or on top of its cage, and an opened door, and that could well be the last time you see your pet bird. In essence, the decision to keep a tame pet bird fully flighted should not be taken lightly. You must secure your bird's environment so no opportunity exists for it to fly

The structure of a lovebird's wing.

out a door or window. Remember that you alone may not control the environment. If you have children or frequent visitors, these will add factors that you may not be able to control at all times.

Other issues in homes with fully flighted birds are ceiling fans and open toilets. A fully flighted bird can more easily get high enough to be hit by the fan or far enough to end up in a bathroom. The latter can be a hazard for clipped birds as well.

Homes that can properly care for fully flighted birds have a room that does not allow access to the outdoors directly. The windows and doors are protected with strong screens, and birds are never allowed

- Primaries
- Greater coverts
- Wing coverts
- Bastard wing, alula or winglet
- Bend of wing
- Lesser and median wing coverts
- Speculum
- Secondaries
- Shoulder
- Tertiaries (flight feathers)

to move about unsupervised so they could chew through the screens. These rooms are located in an area of the home where no visitors or absentminded member of the family could inadvertently let your bird escape.

It my experience, most homes are not set up this way. The first problem with this scenario is often that such a room will probably not be in the most socially active part of the house. Because birds are flock creatures, they will not be happy if they are on their own in a back room.

How Clipping Affects Training

By far the most effective means of training a wild or terrified bird is first to clip its wings. If your bird is flying madly around the room crashing into walls to escape handling, it can seriously injure itself. Chasing a bird with a net certainly does nothing to improve the bond between you and your pet. Chapter 6, "Behavior and Training," will discuss this further.

Toxins and Fumes

A bird's lungs are quite different from human lungs or those of cats and dogs.

Whereas human lungs act like balloons, filling up with air, birds have air sacs that hold the air then move it through the lungs. The air returns to the air sacs before exiting as well. For this reason, their lungs can get much more oxygen, which helps them when they are flying long distances. However, the structure of their lungs makes them uniquely susceptible to airborne fumes and toxins, much more so than humans. The air sacs can be easily damaged by contaminants, so it is extremely important that you not expose your bird to anything that could compromise its breathing system.

Canaries were used in coal mines to detect the presence of deadly fumes for a good reason: they succumb to fumes much sooner than a human would. Therefore, what might not be sufficiently toxic for a human even to feel symptoms of distress can quickly kill a bird.

The list of substances that could possibly kill your bird is a long one. Unfortunately, most people have discovered the dangers of these fumes the hard way: by losing their bird. When an avian veterinarian performs a necropsy on such a bird, he or she will usually see severe damage to the air sacs, such as hemorrhaging or tissue destruction. Obviously, this is a very painful way to die and should be avoided with the utmost vigilance.

Nonstick Cookware

One of the greatest dangers to the lungs and air sacs of pet birds is overheated nonstick cookware. This comes in a variety of brand names, such as Teflon and Silverstone. Some manufacturers now add to their cookware warning tags that explain how overheating these pans can endanger pet birds. When nonstick cookware is overheated, it releases polytetrafluoroethylene (PTFE) fumes, the polymer used to create the nonstick surface. Deaths among birds due to inhalation of these fumes are well documented in veterinary literature. Some tragic incidents have resulted in the loss of whole flocks in a home due to hidden nonstick surfaces in space heaters and other household items such as irons and blow-dryers. Therefore, knowing which of your appliances may have hidden nonstick surfaces is important. If you are not sure, never use these items in a room in which your bird shares the airspace or in a room where fumes could be ventilated into a bird's living area.

Most deaths of pet birds exposed to overheated nonstick cookware have not been in homes where the owners did not know the dangers. In most cases, the people were fully aware of the dangers but believed they could safely use the pans in the home. They then had a single incident where they were distracted for a few minutes. In one case, the owner was boiling water for hot chocolate and forgot the pan was on the stove. In another incident, the owner answered the phone and lost track of the time. A few minutes later, the owner realized the mistake when he heard or saw the bird fall off its perch and succumb to the invisible fumes. Exposure to these fumes is usually fatal. In cases where it is not fatal due to only slight exposure, the lungs and air sacs will

Toxic Fumes to Avoid
- Overheated cooking oil
- Cooking bag fumes
- Aerosol cleaners
- Air fresheners
- Scented cleaners
- Pine-scented items
- New carpet fumes (formaldehyde)
- Carpet powders and cleaners
- Scented toilet paper or tissue (unscented are fine)
- Leather protectant sprays
- Wax potpourri (dry potpourri if eaten)
- Glue guns

be permanently compromised because no treatment can reverse the damage.

In homes where birds are kept near kitchens, often the best policy is to have stainless steel cookware. Certain PTFE-coated cookware, such as oven drip pans, should never be used in homes with birds because even under normal cooking conditions, they reach temperatures high enough to release PTFE fumes. If you know you burn a pan at least once a month out of inattention or forgetfulness, nonstick cookware can be a real danger in your home. An interesting final point is that these fumes also cause a reaction in humans. This has been informally referred to as Teflon fever in the scientific literature. However, humans have much greater defenses against such exposure, so it merely results in a fever and symptoms that some-

Other Hazardous Items

- Glass beads
- Electric cords
- Linoleum (lead poisoning if chewed)
- Old paint (lead based)
- Halogen lamps with open tops
- Cushions on couches (hiding places)
- Polyvinyl chloride (soft PVC items)
- Cedar bedding (toxic to birds)
- Vacuum cleaners

what resemble the early stages of the flu. A study on rats found, "PTFE fumes containing ultrafine particles initiate a severe inflammatory response at low inhaled particle mass concentrations, which is suggestive of an oxidative injury."[3]

Scented Candles and Other Fumes

A number of anecdotal cases exist of birds dying after exposure to scented items. Scented candles, heated essential oils, and plug-in air fresheners are all items that owners have reported using and then seeing a deadly effect on their birds. If you must use these items, use them judiciously, always protecting your bird from exposure to the actual scented fumes.

---

[3]Johnston C. J., Finkelstein J. N., Gelein R., Baggs R., Oberdorster G. "Characterization of the early pulmonary inflammatory response associated with TPFE fume exposure." *Toxicol Appl Pharmacol,* 140(1):154–63, Sept. 1996.

Drafts

A drafty room is not the same thing as a cold room. A draft is a thread of air that leaks through a window or other opening that is significantly cooler than the ambient room temperature. If your bird is unable to move away from a draft because of the location of its cage, this can cause respiratory illness and even death. Move your hand around the edges of any window or door near your bird's cage to make sure no drafts will affect the area where it sits. Additionally, do not set your bird's cage in an area that is in direct line with a strong cross breeze.

Other Household Dangers

In addition to ceiling fans and open toilets, a bird can get injured in the home in a number of other ways. If your bird is properly supervised when out of its cage, you can avoid most of these dangers. Any open container with water can be a hazard for your bird. In one case, a budgie drowned in a glass of wine. Pots and pans being heated on the stove can create a terrible hazard. In a number of stories, birds have fluttered off a shoulder and into a pot. In one incident, the bird flew into boiling tomato sauce. Put your bird into its cage when you are cooking, and do not make an exception to this rule.

Floor Walkers

Floor walkers are birds that like to climb down off their play stand or cage and wander around the house looking for their human flock. Floor walkers put themselves in a position to be crushed. This behavior should absolutely never be allowed. It is extremely dangerous, and many a bird has been lost to this type of accident. This can also create aggression as floor walkers often become toe biters.

Dangerous Toys

Just because a toy was specifically manufactured for a bird does not mean it is safe for all birds. A toy must be the appropriate size for your bird. For example, a plastic chain with spacing just wide enough for a head to go in, but not come back out, could result in the bird hanging itself. This is true of rope toys as well. Rope toys should also be trimmed regularly, as should the bird's toenails, to avoid trapping toenails or feet in the threads. One lovebird chewed its own toes off to escape from such strings. This bird managed to get around quite well after the incident but could have easily bled to death if the owner had not been quick to react and treat the bird.

Use your judgment when giving a bird a toy. Do not assume it is safe. If you suspect your bird is playing with it in a way that could be hazardous, remove the toy immediately. Lanyard clips that are used to hang toys from a cage can be safe for many birds, but some birds will chew on them and risk getting the edge of the metal clip lodged in their beak. If you see your bird play with the actual clip, remove it and get a quick-link type clip to attach the toy to the cage.

Other toys that have had incidents associated with them include the following: metal chains where the links were not properly closed, which can allow a toenail to get stuck in the spacing; rope perches with loose strings; cage covers with loose strings; balls with holes and a bell inside that are traditionally given to cats, which can trap a bird's beak or head; and cages where the door can be pushed up and that can then possibly land on the bird's neck and trap it in this deadly position.

A special warning should be made about furry sleeping huts. I have personally received reports of three accidents, two resulting in death, associated with these items. In one case, the bird died unexpectedly. Necropsy revealed an impaction due to ingestion of the bright, furry material covering a sleeping hut. In another case, the bird had chewed a hole in the center of the hut where the owner did not notice it; the bird got its head stuck in this hole and was strangled. The nonfatal case was of an African grey who ended up having two toes amputated due to the severe blood loss after its leg was trapped in loose material. The vast majority of birds will safely enjoy these items. Once again, the individual owner has the responsibility to monitor the bird's interaction with this cage accessory and determine if it is safe for the bird.

Flavored woods are another popular pet toy you should avoid. The fruity flavors encourage ingestion; the sharp shards of splintered wood can do damage to the bird's digestive system. Dyed wood is fine since flavorless food coloring is used.

Some toys may contain zinc or lead, which can cause heavy metal poisoning very quickly in small parrots. This is addressed more specifically in Chapter 4, "Avian Health."

Lovebirds love to chew. Always remember that lovebirds are great chewers. They will wholeheartedly chew just about anything they can get their beaks around. Get your bird toys that allow it to exercise its beak. Make sure it is not entertaining itself by chewing your books, furniture, or other household items. Vegetable-tanned leather strips are an excellent addition to a lovebird's cage. Your bird will thoroughly enjoy chewing these items. These can also be used to distract your bird from chewing on you or your clothing when it is out playing. If you do not give your lovebird safe items to chew, it will be looking for any alternative. I have seen lovebirds chew right through their wood perches; they have quite confused looks on their faces when they chew through that last piece and drop to the floor of the cage.

Sleeping with Your Bird

Absolutely, positively never even consider sleeping with your bird. You cannot control your movements when you sleep, and your body weight would suffocate a bird in just a few seconds. In a number of incidents in which owners slept with their birds, they experienced the tragic consequences of this irresponsible behavior.

Birds and Cats

Many a time I have heard joyous owners relate how well their cat gets along with their bird. They will tell how the bird rides around on the cat's back or how they sit side by side on the couch. While not having an antagonistic situation of predator and prey in your cat-and-bird home might be a pleasant surprise, allowing any interaction between these two different creatures is extremely unwise. Cats carry a bacteria that is a normal part of their flora, *Pasteurella*. While this does no harm to them, it is deadly to birds. If ever your bird is even gently batted by a cat, you must get the bird to an avian veterinarian immediately. If your bird is infected with this bacterium, it can succumb to infection in a matter of days.

Other Pets in the Home

In many homes, multiple creatures dwell in relative harmony. However, because birds are small, delicate, and usually not fully flighted, you must take extra precautions to ensure their safety in any home with nonbird pets. Although many dogs get along fine with birds, some species struggle with their presence. Any species bred to capture birds, such as retriever-type dogs, or to capture small animals, such as terriers, present a much higher risk to birds. Their natural instincts can kick in if startled by a bird fluttering to the floor. People who keep dogs and cats in the home with a bird need to be doubly sure that the birds are supervised at all times. Cages should be secured in such a way that they cannot be knocked to the floor by an overly zealous dog or cat.

Ferrets can be an extreme hazard in homes with birds. Ferrets are a natural predator to birds and should never be allowed to play in any area where you keep your pet birds. This is also true of large snakes. In the wild, snakes are one of the few predators of birds other than humans. Needless to say, it would be a high-anxiety environment for any bird where a snake dwells in close proximity.

Children and Birds

Small children can unfortunately be a great hazard to small birds. Children under five years of age can be impulsive and inadvertently careless. They move quickly, which makes most birds nervous, and they sometimes become overexcited, knocking over cages or tripping to the floor with a little bird clutched against their bodies. Most children under the age of seven should be supervised at all times if they are handling your bird. Take even more care with children under the age of five. Specifically purchasing a lovebird for a child under age seven is probably not a good idea unless the child is particularly mature and responsible.

When a Bird Escapes

Nothing is quite like the feeling a person gets when he or she watches the beloved pet bird suddenly fly off, disappearing over rooftops and trees. The best thing to do is to prevent a fly-away in the first place because owners who lose their birds this way usually do not get them back. Keeping the wings trimmed is obviously the best prevention. However, many times it is the birds who are normally clipped who end up flying off. Flight feathers can grow in quickly, particularly in young birds or birds who are currently molting. Because lovebirds are small, all they need are a few flight feathers for them to get sufficient lift. For this reason, you must be very observant and recognize when your bird is getting sufficient lift to take off. Take into consideration your particular environment as well. For example, if you live on a hill in a windy area, you are at much higher risk of a partially flighted bird covering great distances quickly.

Even this clipped bird has regrown enough flight feathers to get significant lift.

Many an owner has been sadly surprised to see what he or she thought was a clipped bird disappear on the horizon.

If you notice your bird getting lift, the time has come for another wing trim. Remember that young birds may need their wings trimmed in as few as four to six weeks. If you cannot take your bird in for its wing trim right away, do not ever open the door or a window if the bird is riding around on your shoulder or sitting out on its cage. If you know you have gone past the prime period in which you should get a wing trim, do not take your bird outside with you under any circumstances. In at least half a dozen stories, birds that "would never leave my side" have been startled by a crow flying overhead or a car backfiring. Most of these owners never saw their birds again.

To ensure the return of your pet should it ever escape, make sure you have some clear photographs on hand. If the bird has a band on the leg, write down the information so you will have it available should you be asked to identify the bird.

After an Escape

It is my hope that after reading the previous section, you will not ever have a need for this information. However, this is unrealistic, and many birds will still end up escaping from homes. Your first reaction will most likely be panic. If you can see your bird, try to get someone to watch it while you get its favorite treat or its cage. You want to have your eye on this bird at all times in case it flies again. If you do not know the general direction your bird flew in, tracking it down can be impossible.

A bird that does not normally fly may simply not know how to get back to you. It may be chirping at you and want to be retrieved, but you may be unable to reach your bird. If its wings are not fully grown in, it may not feel secure enough even to try flying to you. The big outdoors can be quite overwhelming for a bird that is used to a room with four walls. It may become confused and frightened. If it panics, it may end up even farther away from your home. Sometimes placing the bird's cage where it can see it helps. This is perceived as home and might entice the bird to come down from its high perch. If you have a mate for this particular bird, bring it out in a secure cage and set it where the two can see and hear each other. If you do happen to retrieve your bird, move slowly and calmly. The bird will be very nervous and hypervigilant. If you move your hands too quickly to grab it, the bird could fly off again. Even the tamest of birds can overreact under these circumstances. You need to put yourself into its position and understand how frightening the experience can be.

Posting Signs

If your bird is nowhere to be found, the most important thing to do next is to get signs up in the neighborhood. A tame lovebird will often go to a human, sometimes the first human it sees. If you have posted a picture of your bird in the neighborhood, a person who has found your bird may give you a call and return it. However, if your bird is particularly sweet, some people will simply keep it. This is unfortunate. Although many people would not think twice about returning a lost cat or dog, they seem to feel a lost bird is fair game to keep. Beware of offering rewards up front for a found bird. Some scam artists will pretend they have your bird. You can usually detect such scams when the person tries to get you to meet them in an unusual location. Never go to a strange place, especially a place that is not public, to get your bird. Another way to prevent people from taking advantage of your situation is to withhold some details about the bird. For example, if the bird has a band, do not give the band information on the poster or advertisement about your missing bird. Anyone claiming to have your bird should be able to give you this information.

Sometimes walking around your neighborhood and knocking on doors can be useful. However, this can prove fruitless if the bird has flown away from the immediate area. Most lovebirds are strong, fast fliers and can end up many miles away in a short time. Putting posters up at local veterinarian offices, pet stores, and even coffee shops is also a good idea. In one instance, a cockatiel was returned to an owner weeks after escaping because someone saw his lost-bird poster in a local bakery. Many online resources are available for posting lost and/or found bird notices, the most popular being *http://www.birdhotline.com*.

Chapter Six

Behavior and Training

Lovebirds Are Parrots

The most important thing to recognize about lovebirds is that they are indeed parrots. Because of this, they are extremely intelligent and, at times, willful. Treat your lovebird the way you would any parrot, even though it is much smaller than many parrot species. Issues such as dominance, cage territoriality, and nippiness can develop in lovebirds if you do not take the proper steps to prevent these behaviors. This means you must begin the training process the first day you bring your bird home.

Gentle Dominance

The idea of gentle dominance has become very popular in recent years due to the work of avian behaviorists. However, the phrase has evolved over the years and can mean differ-

Many people believe that blue mutation peachfaced lovebirds tend to be calmer than wild-colored (normal) lovebirds, but color does not generally affect temperament.

ent things to different people. Basically, gentle dominance means that you assert you are head of the flock through persuasion and positive interaction, never frightening, intimidating, or physically punishing the bird. You can be in charge of your flock, which can be even a single bird, only if the flock trusts you. Consistent, positive interaction creates the greatest bonds of trust.

What Not to Do, Ever

Do not ever flick or pull on your bird's beak. Do not ever slap or hit your bird. These might seem like obvious rules, but some frustrated bird owners have overreacted to an unexpected bite in these ways. Dropping your bird to the floor after a bite is a highly ineffective way of training. It merely teaches your lovebird that you are an unreliable perch that cannot be trusted. The bird might be shocked into temporary submission but might not be so eager to step up onto your hand the next time you put it into the cage.

Aggressive training methods are simply lazy training methods. Even screaming at your bird can merely antagonize it and cause it to act more aggressively. In fact, if your bird has developed an annoying habit of screaming or calling obsessively, chances are you reinforced this by reacting, either by screaming or by using some other deterrent. Some people will hit the cage or shake it to stop the noise, but this is interaction. Just like a two-year-old child, any interaction is better than no interaction. You will find these tactics merely increase the behaviors rather than stop them.

The *Step-up* Command

The most essential trick to teach your lovebird is to step up on command. You can say, *"Step-up"* or *"Up up,"* but use the same command consistently whenever you pick up your bird. The *step-up* command must be used on every occasion you pick up your bird, without exception. By following this simple rule, you set the groundwork for long-term, positive interaction with your lovebird.

The *step-up* command is particularly important when removing your bird from its cage. Allowing a bird just to climb out of the cage on its own can create cage territoriality issues in the future. The best method of removal is to put your finger against the chest of your bird and gently press while giving the *up* command. Always make strong eye contact with your bird whenever you give this or any other verbal instruction.

If you have already developed a problem with your bird biting or refusing to come out of the cage, you may have to pick it up bodily. After removing the bird, you should practice the *step-up* command by having it step up from one hand to the other a few times. Do not overdo these practice sessions. Have the bird step from one finger to the next about four or five times, then reward your bird with praise. You can also occasionally reward it with a favorite treat. Take breaks between these *step-up* training sessions, then practice again a few minutes later. You can then practice having your bird step down onto its play stand or cage and then up again onto your finger. Have patience when doing this exercise and give only positive reinforcement when your bird makes the attempt to step up. Young lovebirds will often learn this trick in a day or so.

Hand Shy

If you are already in a situation where your lovebird bites when you reach into the cage, you may have become hand shy: you pull your hand away as soon as you see the beak go down. A few good bites will make anyone nervous about offering a finger to that strong beak. However, lovebirds use their beak like a third hand to help them balance. By pulling your hand away, you give your bird the message that you are an unreliable perch. If this situation currently exists, retrieving your bird with a towel and then working on the *step-up* command outside the cage may be best. However, this can in itself create issues. So if you can simply reach in and pick up the bird quickly, this is preferable to using a towel. Do not chase your bird around the cage. Be quick and decisive, and get the bird out. You are far less likely to be bitten once you have gotten the bird away from its primary territory.

Some birds respond well to stick training. This is when you use the *step-up* command but have the bird step onto a wooden dowel at first when removing it from the cage. This should be only a temporary measure if you have become hand shy, because what you really want is a bird that willingly steps up onto your hand as soon as you reach into the cage. You simply use the perch the same way you would your finger, pressing it gently against the chest until the bird steps onto it. If the stick sends your bird into a wild panic, this technique may not work, although most birds will usually become accustomed to the dowel in a few days. However, you do not want to chase your bird around the cage with the stick. This is counterproductive and can sabotage your efforts to train your bird.

Many people make the common mistake of dropping the *up* command once they feel their bird is

A breeder who handles baby birds from a young age will raise birds who are not afraid of hands.

coming out of the cage easily. This command should be used consistently throughout the life of your bird to reinforce the behavior continually.

Power Plays

The high intelligence of these little birds means that they can often figure out how to manipulate their owners. The main response they are working for is attention, plain and simple. Even after you have established dominance, you must continue to maintain the pecking order with verbal and visual cues. Many lovebirds will learn ways to manipulate their owners. Some common tricks are to slam the cage door up and down, call incessantly, or run back and forth along the front of the cage in a manner that seems desperate. The goal of all these behaviors is to get your attention. If you give the bird either positive or negative attention in response to these behaviors, you will reinforce the behavior.

If you listen to your lovebird, you will get to a point where you understand certain vocalizations. One particular type of call is known as the contact call. This is used in the wild when flock members want to touch base with each other or locate other birds in their group. Often, the simplest way to avoid the development of a screaming problem is to answer the initial contact call quietly with a simple, "I'm right here." Using the same phrase is helpful. In fact, using the same phrase in response to any activity increases the chances of your bird actually learning to mimic the phrase. If your bird continues to call after you have answered, often the best response is no response at all. Of course, if this call has a sound of alarm to it or is something you have never heard before, always check to make sure the bird is not injured or in need of help. Do not worry about being tricked by your bird a few times. You will quickly get to know which calls are meant to manipulate you, and you can then use the tactic of ignoring that particular noise. As you become more familiar with your lovebird's vocalizations, you will instinctively know when you must react and make sure your bird is fine.

Lovebirds vocalize to keep in contact with the flock and communicate. Their singsong chirping in the morning and the evening is an instinctive flock behavior done in the wild. You might say this is their way of communicating the day is beginning and the day is winding down. Most likely, these communal symphonies of chirping in the evening would be a way for lovebirds who are off searching for food to find the flock before sunset. Anyone who is interested in keeping a bird as a pet should understand that vocalizations will be a natural part of their bird's behavior. As long as the owner understands this behavior, he or she can avoid reinforcing negative expressions, such as constant squawking.

Another typical power play is refusing to go back into the cage. A good way to reinforce the bird's compliance when you want it to return to its home is simply to practice. Take your bird out for short play periods and put it back into its cage, praising the bird as you do so. You can also use a *step-down* command to place your bird onto its perch. Take the bird out again a little while later and repeat this process. In most cases, the problem of a bird refusing to go back into the cage is in a home where it is played with only once a day for an extended period. Short playtimes, sometimes even periods only five minutes long throughout the day or evening, can help alleviate this issue. Do not wait until you have a large block of time

Case Study: A Masked Lovebird with an Annoying Call

A man e-mailed me complaining about a 13-month-old lovebird that had started to develop a repetitious, annoying noise at around 8 months of age. It was not a sound native to this species. The bird would make the sound endlessly. This bird had also learned some words, which the owner enjoyed. The bird made this incessant noise only when it was in its cage.

I explained to the owner that the bird most likely picked this noise up from the environment, either from outside birds or something mechanical, such as a truck's back-up beep or another, similar humanmade noise. My suggestion was to ignore the noise completely and not react to it in any way. He should not look at the bird when it makes the noise; in fact, he should act as if the bird's noise does not reach him at all. Whenever the bird stops making the noise for a few moments, the owner should go over and praise it and even take the bird out to interact with him for a moment. The goal is to teach the bird that this sound will not get a reaction. The noise will become useless to it, and it will lose interest in recreating the noise.

At first the owner was dubious. He wrote that he did not think ignoring the sound was possible because it was maddening. I told him that although it might seem impossible in the short run, he will most likely be happy with the result.

One month later I received an e-mail from the owner, who was overjoyed at the effectiveness of this method. The lovebird rarely made the noise anymore. When it did, the noise lasted only a few seconds. In fact, the owner believed the bird actually seemed happier now. The other nice aftereffect of this training was that the bird started to vocalize normally more and began using more words and phrases to communicate. By positively reinforcing the sounds the owner wanted to hear, the bird had learned how to live best with its flock.

Blue and black masked lovebirds.

to handle your bird. If you have two minutes, take those two minutes to pick your bird up and talk to it. It will come to understand then that going back into the cage does not necessarily mean it cannot come out again until the next day.

Sometimes your bird will maniacally pace back and forth in front of the cage door as if desperately begging you to let it out. This behavior, along with repetitive lifting and dropping of a door to get your attention, is best ignored. If you react to these behaviors, you can reinforce them to a point where they will become annoying, not to mention exhausting for the bird. You should also take note as to whether or not your bird is able to lift the door up and stick its head through. Lovebirds are well-known escape artists. Should the bird get out when you are not home, this could be dangerous. Even worse, if the bird gets only its head out and the door comes back down, it could get trapped and strangle itself while struggling to get free.

How Nibbling Turns to Biting

One of the most common e-mails I receive are about sweet, hand-raised lovebirds who all of a sudden started biting one day for no apparent reason. In almost all cases when the owners are questioned, I learn that the bird had been allowed to nibble gently on their earlobes, neck, or fingers for many months before the hard biting ever started. It is a fact that nibbling almost always turns to biting if allowed to continue. By discouraging any sort of nibbling on your body, you can prevent it from developing into biting.

A good method for stopping the nibbling behavior is to provide a distraction. For example, vegetable-tanned leather strips can be held near the bird so it chews that rather than you. Unscented tissues rolled up also seem to be a favorite for lovebirds to shred. Lovebirds are chewers by nature, so you need to direct this behavior in a direction that is acceptable to you.

If this method does not alleviate the problem you can *gently* move your lovebird's beak way from your skin and give a firm command, *"No biting!"* The beak is very sensitive, so you do not need to pull it. If the bird persists, give it three chances, then put it back into the cage for five minutes. After that short rest period, take the bird out and start over. This process can seem frustrating at first. However, if you are consistent with your cues and behavior and are patient, most lovebirds will learn the rules.

Biting and Tired Birds

Many people notice that their lovebirds are very sweet and playful for about 20 or 30 minutes and then seem to become irritable and nippy after that. They try to figure out how to stop the behavior by saying *"No"* or moving the bird's beak away.

They are missing the very simple solution to this problem, which is to put the bird back into its cage before it gets to the point of being irritable and nippy. Lovebirds have fast metabolisms and are very energetic. Giving your bird a break from play to go eat and drink will usually stop this problem completely. As humans we certainly know how tired and grumpy we get when we stay with a task too long. The same applies to lovebirds, although their attention spans are shorter and their rest requirements tend to be greater.

Entrenched Biting

If you adopt an older lovebird that has not been handled for some time, it may have a serious biting habit that can be difficult to turn around. Lovebirds bite most often for two basic reasons: they are frightened or upset. Causes for fright might be a stranger in the room or some sudden movement or event. Many people feel this is their bird's way of warning them that danger is present. In some cases, owners feel their birds are jealous of another person in the room. Lovebirds that are not handled regularly or are neglected or abused will also develop biting as a defense. If you regularly play with your bird at the beginning and then become too busy to make time for it, the bird may bite to express its frustration when you finally take it out to play.

If your lovebird has decided you are its one and only, it may start to become aggressive toward other family members. Preventing this situation from the beginning is best. Make sure all family members handle the bird. Also have other family members take part in feeding and cage cleaning. If an issue has already developed, you can do short practice sessions where you have other family members take the bird from you using the *up* command. You can help by also telling the bird to step up onto the other person's hand. Praise the bird when it obeys. At first, take the bird back right away using the *up* command. You can increase the time with the other person as you practice this over a few days or weeks. This type of jealousy biting is best dealt with as soon as you notice the problem. If you let it develop into full-blown aggression toward others, you may have a situation where family members want nothing to do with the bird and refuse to be in the room when the bird is out of its cage.

The Broody Hen

A particular issue with pet lovebirds can occur when a hen decides she absolutely must breed. Without a mate, one of its owners will become the primary target of this behavior. You may notice your bird dipping its feathers down as if exposing the rump area. That is exactly what she is doing. This is the position hens take when they want the male to mate with them. The male would climb onto her lower back, sometimes holding the flight feathers for grip. This is how the hen's eggs are fertilized. When you have a single pet hen, this can be amusing at first. However, if she starts protecting her cage and laying egg after egg, you could end up with a problem. It is best to avoid triggering this behavior and remove anything from the cage that might encourage nesting.

The first behaviors you might notice are nest-seeking behaviors. This might include the shredding of paper on the bottom of the cage, a tendency to want to hide in your shirt, or sometimes crouching under an elevated seed dish. Remember that in the wild, most lovebird species use holes in trees, rocks, or buildings to build their nests. So they crave dark, cavelike places when the instinct to breed kicks in. The next behavior you might notice will be how protective the hen becomes of this area. For example, you might reach into your shirt to retrieve her and suddenly you get a nasty bite. This is typical behavior for a broody hen who has a strong instinct to reproduce.

The most important thing to do when you first notice these behaviors is to avoid triggering them. A hen exhibiting such signs should not have hiding places in the cage such as sleeping huts. Do not let the hen climb into your shirt. Having a cage with a grated bottom that separates the bird from the paper liner is best. This way, the hen is not constantly building nests on the bottom of the cage by shredding this paper. Do not encourage any kind of nest-building behavior. This will only result in a hen settling in to lay dud eggs. It needlessly wastes her energy and can make for a very nasty, unreasonable pet. The hen will think of you as her mate and will expect you to act accordingly. Obviously, this is impossible, so she may take out her frustration on you by biting.

Invariably, a hen exhibiting these behaviors will at some point lay an egg. Even if you take steps to avoid triggering this, it is a very strong instinct and there is not much you can do about it. However, you should take great care to make sure your hen does not damage her health by laying egg after infertile egg. Make sure she has a cuttlebone available for calcium supplementation. You should also do what you can to redirect her energies.

You can do two things with these eggs. What works can vary from bird to bird. The first method is to let the egg sit for a day or two and then remove it. Many people feel guilty about removing the egg. However, if you leave the egg in the cage, the hen may start to lay more eggs to fill out the clutch. She will waste an enormous amount of energy sitting on eggs that will never hatch. The second method is simply to leave the eggs, let the hen finish out the clutch (five or six eggs), and let her sit on them for the usual incubation period for that species. People who do this have found that by removing the egg, it triggers more egg-laying behavior.

Cobalt blue and blue peachfaced lovebirds.

I have personally found that leaving the egg in there is much more of a trigger than removing it. If you remove the egg within the first day or so, chances are the hen will lay another egg or two. However, if you keep removing them, she loses interest and stops in most cases. Remember, once a hen lays an egg, her body is already gearing up to develop another one. Therefore, one egg almost always means two eggs. You do not have to rush in and remove the egg the moment she lays it, but I generally remove it within the first few days after it was laid.

The process of developing the egg, laying it, and brooding takes an enormous amount of energy. Your hen should be on a very healthy diet. You should also make sure she has sufficient calcium to make up for the large amount used by her body to develop the shell of the egg. If she insists upon laying many eggs (over six in a one-month period), you can take a few steps. First, change her immediate environment. Remove the hen from the cage, and put her into a temporary holding cage. Put her into a room where she cannot see what you are doing. Remove all the perches and toys from the cage, and completely remodel her home. Put in new perches, move them to new locations, add a new toy, and even rearrange her food dishes. You might even consider moving her cage to a slightly different location. Once the cage is totally refurbished, bring the hen back out and let her go into her new home. Often, this will redirect her behavior away from persistent egg laying. She will be more concerned about getting to know her new home.

The longer days of spring can often trigger nesting behavior, as can unseasonably warm spells in the midst of fall or winter. If you can simulate the longer days of winter by using a bird-safe cage cover, you can avoid the natural trigger of long days. Make sure your hen gets at least ten hours of dark sleep time. If you keep your bird in a room where family members watch television late at night, a dark, bird-safe cage cover will allow her to go to sleep while you stay up. The longer it is light out, the more likely a bird is to go into a breeding cycle.

If your hen is persistent, laying numerous eggs and challenging your patience, take her to an avian veteriniarian. In extreme cases where the hen could be compromising her health, veterinarians can give a shot that reduces the hormones that trigger the breeding cycle. If she has laid an enormous number of eggs (ten or more) in a short period of time, you may want to ask about a liquid calcium supplement. This is given orally twice a day and is intended for hens who have had a problem passing eggs. It helps to bring up their calcium levels more quickly than ordinary dietary supplements.

Egg Binding

If your hen is laying eggs, you do need to be very aware of her health. If she appears lethargic, puffed up, or is not eating, the first thing to do is turn her over and see if her vent is swollen. She could be having a problem passing an egg. Then you need to get the bird warm. Put her into a brooder as described in Chapter 4, "Avian Health."

Once she is settled, call your avian veterinarian immediately and tell him or her you have a hen who appears to be egg bound and that it is an emergency. Egg-bound hens will generally die within 24 to 48 hours if not given proper medical attention. Handle her gently. If the egg breaks inside her, she is at risk for egg peritonitis, which has a very high mortality rate. In most cases, this kind of situation can be avoided with proper nutrition and by taking steps to discourage egg-laying behavior.

Is This Normal?

Lovebirds can sometimes exhibit what appears to be very odd behavior. They might hang from the top of the cage and start bobbing. I have one lovebird who sits on the top of his swing and hits the bell, squealing as if another bird is attacking him. Many times I have come into the room to see if some birds are fighting, only to see this battle between Wolf and his bell. Saying what is normal for your particular lovebird is hard. I have yet to find two lovebirds whose behavior is exactly alike.

One behavior that some owners find disconcerting is rubbing on the perches or toys in the cage. Most likely if you see this behavior you have a male. This is an instinctive sexual behavior, and is totally normal. You may notice an increase in frequency during certain times of the year, especially when cold weather first starts to turn warm. Some males do this rarely; some seem to make it one of their primary activities. It is a way for them to release frustration. Spraying a male bird with water or otherwise punishing for this behavior is a waste of time. It is completely natural. One parent finally gave up trying to hide this behavior and actually used it to broach the subject of the birds and the bees with her son. For both hens and males, you can avoid stimulating these types of behaviors when they are out of the cage by not petting the rump area. Males will also sometimes regurgitate for their owner the same way they would for their mate. Just be sure that this is merely a mating behavior. If you see any signs of illness, this could be due to something other than affection toward you.

Talking and Tricks

Lovebirds can learn quickly if behaviors are positively reinforced. Often the opportunity to teach a trick can be when the bird does something spontaneously and you react to it. Your bird will often remember the reaction and want to repeat the trick. If you then attach a word to it, you create a cue for the actual trick. For example, a bird might push a ball around. You can praise the bird and say the phrase, *"Roll the ball!"* You want to use the same phrase each time the bird repeats the behavior.

If you are determined to teach tricks, you may want to get a separate stand for your bird so you can work away from the cage. A stand with various ladders and toys can be very enjoyable for a lovebird. What tricks you may be able to teach your bird will be determined by your observation of its natural behaviors, consistent and positive reinforcement of particular behaviors you would like to see repeated, the development of verbal and visual cues, and patience.

One trick that can be taught if started with a very young lovebird is to have the bird lie upside down on your hand. You must begin slowly because this is not a natural position for it. Let the bird continue to grip your fingers with its feet the first few times you do this. Only do this for a few seconds, and attach a specific phrase and praise to it. You might say, *"Go on your back. Good bird!"* Do not push the bird beyond its limits of comfort for this trick. In fact, some birds simply will not accept the idea, and you should not force the issue. However, if you start with a very young bird that was recently weaned, you may be able to teach this trick. Move slowly and calmly. Stroke the top of the bird's crown.

A curious peachfaced baby explores its environment.

After a few days of doing this for a few seconds at a time on a number of occasions, you can try to get the bird to release the grip with one foot. Start with only one foot at first, and work on this position for a few days. Stroking the head will relax your bird. Some birds go into an almost trancelike state if the owner makes circular movements on the crown of the head and around the eyes with a finger. Again, never have the bird hold the position for more than a few seconds. The next step is to work on getting the bird to relax the grip with both feet. This is an important step because if you push it too quickly or try to force the issue, you could end up losing the progress you have already established. Again, once the bird releases so that neither foot is gripping you, praise it and bring it back to the perch position.

Patience and understanding are essential in teaching such tricks. Never put trick training over the happiness of your bird. You should not force your bird to amuse you at the expense of its feelings of security and safety. Remember that some birds will not respond to trick training as well as others. You, as a compassionate owner, must recognize when this type of training frustrates or irritates your bird in such a way that you should not persist in trying.

A cute and easy trick to teach can be done with a very simple prop, the inner cardboard roll of unscented toilet paper rolls. First, be sure this is unscented toilet paper as some reports have indicated that the scented papers can make birds sick. Put the roll onto the floor of the cage. The bird will explore it, sometimes destroying it with its beak. However, many lovebirds will crawl inside the roll. Some groups of baby lovebirds have let each one take a turn climbing in the roll while the others push it around. This can be a very amusing trick that requires very little effort on your part. Make sure your particular lovebird is not too big for the cardboard roll. If you are at all concerned that your bird could get trapped in the roll, remove the toy when you are not supervising your bird.

Lovebirds and Speech

All parrots have the potential to mimic. However, not all parrots will learn to mimic. Lovebirds are not as famous for this ability as are some other larger parrot species. However, many owners have related stories of words and phrases their lovebirds repeat. The voice is very low and gruff. Even recognizing that your bird is saying something at first can be difficult. Take note of any particular sounds that are not typical lovebird vocalizations, especially if you hear them on a number of occasions and they seem to be related to some activity or behavior on your part. For example, if every time you approach the cage the bird makes a sound you do not quite recognize, it could be trying to learn something you usually say when you come over to it. Listen carefully, and try to figure out the basic sound.

Repetition within a context is the best way to teach a bird words. Parrots rarely learn words that have no meaning for them. They will say words that relate to their experiences. For example, if every time you approach the cage you say, *"Hi cutie,"* this might be a phrase your bird will attempt to learn. Try to use the same words for a number of activities. Contexts in which a repeated phrase may be learned by a lovebird are when you first come home, when you first come into the room, when you bring fresh foods, when you leave the room or home, and when you take the bird out of the cage. In fact, many parrots learn *"Up up"* as their first phrase when owners use this each and every time they pick up their bird. Some parrots

will say this as you walk by the cage just to see if maybe you will take them up on the offer.

Asking your bird the same questions when you interact can also be a valuable training method. You might ask some of these questions:

"Are you a good bird?"
"Who's the cutie?"
"What are you doing?"
"Want some food?"

For the last question, you should ask this just as you are putting the bowls into the cage. Again, this creates a context for the words, allowing the bird to understand the words' relationship to the activity at that moment. By creating such associations, you increase the chances that the bird will learn a few words.

Lovebirds are parrots, and therefore have the potential to mimic. Many can imitate human sounds such as kisses.

Some Birds Just Do Not Mimic

You should never buy a bird just because you want it to mimic you. No matter how well-known a species is for speaking, not all birds of that species will speak. Lovebirds make wonderful, endearing pets even if they never utter a single human word. If you have the expectation that your bird must speak, you may end up disappointed. Your bird should never be made to feel punished because it does not mimic you.

Of interest to note is that in most cases of particularly good talkers among lovebirds, the birds tended to be hens. For many parrot species, such as budgerigars and Amazons, it is the males who are reportedly the most prolific talkers.

Birds kept in pairs are less likely to imitate human sounds, but in homes where the owner is often away, two birds can keep each other company.

The Importance of Sleep

If you have a lovebird who has become rather grumpy and irritable lately, the first thing to consider is how much sleep it is getting. Birds are much like people in that if they are sleep deprived over a period of time, it will affect their mood and behavior. If your bird is in a part of the house that is lit late at night, it may not get enough shut-eye to fulfill its biological need for sleep. Remember that parrots in the wild roost for the night when the sun goes down and do not start becoming active until first sunrise. In many geographic areas, this can mean 12 hours of darkness or more. If you can mimic the natural light cycles of the environment, your bird will be happier and healthier. A dark, bird-safe cover may help you make sure your bird gets enough dark sleep time. Another solution can be to move the bird into a dark room in the evening, away from a room with bright lights or a blaring television set.

Potty Training

This can be a challenging behavior to teach lovebirds. The main reason it can be difficult is that lovebirds tend to defecate quite often. The first rule of potty training is to know when your bird needs to be given the opportunity to poop in the place where you want it to poop. The first step is to get an idea of

Be sure that any plants in your home or aviary are safe for birds.

how many minutes pass between each time your bird poops. Once you know this time frame, begin to take your bird to the cage or play-stand when you know it is about time for it to poop and give a verbal cue, such as *"Go poop."* You may want to find a phrase that is a little less obvious, but you get the idea. Continue to do this for a number of days. It can be somewhat tiring at first, but many lovebirds will get the idea that they are supposed to poop on the cage or play stand rather than on you. You should also observe what sort of behaviors your bird exhibits right before it poops. Most lovebirds will lean back or even step back a bit and then crouch right before pooping.

If you do this sort of training, you may find that your bird gives you a little warning right before it has to go. If you are observant, you will recognize these signs. Some birds will do a little dance before backing up to let you know it is time for them to go. You can then move them off your clothing and to a place where you want them to defecate. Never force your bird to hold its poops for long periods of time. This sort of training can result in a situation where the bird is so well trained it simply will not go while it is on you. Giving such a bird regular opportunities to go to the area where you want it to poop is only fair. This would be akin to making sure your pet dog has opportunities to go outside when it needs to go.

Chapter Seven
Species and Mutations

The Nine Species

Although there are nine species of lovebird, only a few are available enough to be common as pets. These are the peachfaced, masked, and Fischer's lovebirds. You will sometimes see black-cheeked lovebirds or Abyssinian lovebirds as pets, but not nearly as often. The most popular pet species have a life span that can vary dramatically depending on their diet, care, and general environment. The average life span is 10 to 15 years, but I have heard from owners who have lovebirds well into their 20s.

In terms of availability for breeding purposes, peachfaced, masked, and Fischer's are readily available. Black-cheeked and Abyssinian lovebirds can be found, but they will be more expensive and not as easy to locate. Nyasa and Madagascar lovebirds are very difficult to find in both the United States and Europe. Because of their dwindling numbers in aviculture, the breeding of these birds should be left to more experienced breeders. Red-faced lovebirds are

The pale face on this peachfaced lutino is evidence that this is still a young bird, under six months of age.

extremely difficult to find both in the United States and Europe.

For purposes of this discussion, this text will not go into the details of genetic inheritance when describing the various mutations of each species. Refer to Chapter 9 to understand issues such as sex-linked colors, recessive and dominant genes, and other genetic factors that influence color mutations.

Peachfaced Lovebirds

Peachfaced Lovebirds

Species name: *Agapornis roseicollis roseicollis*

Appearance: The wild-type peachfaced lovebirds have a vibrant green body, a bright red face and bib, and a blue rump. The coverts are green with some blue. The beak

Scientific Classification
Order: Psittaciformes
Family: Psittacidae
Genus: *Agapornis*
Species: *roseicollis, personata, fischeri, nigrigenis, lilianae, cana, taranta, pullaria, swindernia*

Masked lovebird mutations in yellow/ino, white/ino, cobalt, and white.

is horn colored, and the legs are a mottled gray.

Origin: Southwest Africa along coastal plains. They are sometimes seen in the dry plains areas near mountains, but always close to a source of water.

Diet: In the wild, they eat seeds and berries. They are considered a pest in some areas because they will raid agricultural crops.

Sexual dimorphism: No obvious visual differences exist between the sexes.

Breeding: Build nests in holes in cliffs and buildings or take over weaver nests; collect nesting material by tucking it behind the feathers that lay against the rump; lay six eggs on average; incubation lasts 23 days; babies fledge in 43 days. Must have sufficient humidity for eggs to hatch.

I have put this lovebird species into its own category because it is quite different from the eye-ring species and the other non-eye-ring species in many ways. The most commonly seen and by far the most popular lovebird in captivity is the peachfaced lovebird. They are extremely hardy and adaptable birds. Because they are very easy to breed compared with other species, they are abundant in aviculture and the pet bird trade. Hand-fed peachfaced lovebirds that are properly socialized make excellent pets. Such birds are affectionate and devoted to their owners. They also enjoy playing, especially when they have an audience. Many peachfaced lovebirds will swing to and fro from various toys, often taking a quick look over to their human owners to see if they are watching the show. Their sharp

Peachfaced lovebirds are widely available as pets. From top left going clockwise: orangefaced, whitefaced slate, lutino, normal green, and lutino mutations.

calls are rarely offensive to people, although a few people do not like the sound they make. They rarely become a noise problem as long as the rules are established early on and incessant calling is not inadvertently encouraged. See "Behavior and Training," Chapter 6, for more about this topic.

Color Mutations in Peachfaced Lovebirds

A number of beautiful color mutations occur in the peachfaced lovebird that have been developed in aviculture. Remember that these mutated birds are still called peachfaced lovebirds, even in cases where the red psittacin of the face has been reduced or eliminated. Most young lovebirds will have black on their beaks. However, in some mutations, such as pied, this black often does

not show up on the beak. Because of this, breeders can pick out the pied babies in a clutch long before the

The normal peachfaced lovebird is the standard color seen in the wild.

Cobalt, blue, creamino, and dark green mutations of peachfaced lovebirds.

birds have feathers. The colors in both the wild-type and all the mutations do take some time to reach their full vibrancy. You can expect to see some dramatic changes in your bird's color as it matures. A wild-type peachfaced lovebird will have a subtle pinkish red mask for many months, which darkens as the bird matures, especially after the first molt. Lovebirds generally reach their full color around ten months of age. Many mutations occur in this species as well as multiple combinations of these mutations. I will cover only those mutations that are seen most often in pet birds. Some other mutations that occur but are not as readily available among pet peachfaced lovebirds are American yellow, graywing, fallow, lacewing, opaline, and long feather.

Dutch blue, marine, par-blue. A true blue mutation in peachfaced

lovebirds does not exist as it does in the eye-ring species. A blue lovebird is more of a greenish blue bird. The red of the face is dramatically reduced, leaving a creamy bib and a small band over the forehead that is apricot in color. Young babies will appear to have gray heads in this mutation. This gray will fade to the creamy color, and the apricot band across the forehead will begin to become apparent around three months of age. When the color first comes in, it has a mottled appearance. Many breeders refer to this look as the measles stage because of the blotchy way the colors first come in.

Blue is considered to be the ground color, the basic body color. The other mutations can be bred into either green or blue birds. Each mutation will look very different depending on the ground color of the bird. To learn more about ground color and its effect on mutations, refer to Chapter 9.

Pied. A pied lovebird has a dramatic reduction in red psittacine, sometimes eliminating the red face completely. The body color is yellow with variegated greens and greenish blues of different hues. A lightly pied bird will have quite a bit of these variegated colors on the body; a heavily pied bird can be almost completely yellow or have just a few hints of the pied markings on the back where the wings meet.

Pied lovebirds vary dramatically in appearance from one bird to the next, even within the same clutch. If the ground color of the bird is blue,

A lightly pied blue mutation shows very little yellow in the body.

A heavily pied lovebird, sometimes called "clear," shows predominantly yellow on the body.

you will see more shades of the blue-green in the markings.

Ino. An ino bird has a complete absence of melanin, even in the eyes. For this reason, these birds have strikingly beautiful red eyes. If the ground color of the bird is green, the bird will be bright yellow and will retain the bright red face. This is called lutino. If the ground color of the bird is blue, the bird will be a creamy color with hints of yellow. The mask is dramatically reduced, leaving the creamy white bib and a small band of apricot over the forehead. This color is called creamino. A true albino does not occur with peachfaced lovebirds the way it does with eye-ring species. To have a true albino, you would need a true blue bird, which does not yet exist among peachfaced lovebirds.

Australian ino. Although often called Australian cinnamon, this beautiful mutation has a genetic basis similar to that of lutino and creamino. If the ground color of the

Creamino lovebirds are ino mutations with blue ground color. The eyes are red.

American cinnamon has a very different appearance in a bird with green ground color (left) vs. blue ground color (right).

Pied can be bred into most other mutations, although breeding it into ino mutations is discouraged because it causes a jagged edge to the face mask. These are blue pied and blue American cinnamon pied peachfaced lovebirds.

bird is green, you get a vibrant yellow bird with an almost fluorescent lime hue to it; the bird retains the red face. If the ground color is blue, the body has a pale yellow color with a hint of this lime hue. The face mask fades to creamy white, and you will see the apricot band develop over the forehead.

This particular mutation has some unusual characteristics. You can have a male that is split cinnamonino. This means the male is visually an Australian ino, but he is genetically also lutino. Such a male can have both Australian ino and lutino daughters, even if he is put with a hen that does not carry either mutation.

American cinnamon. This mutation is caused by a reduction in black melanin and an increase in brown melanin in the feather structure. The flight feathers on such a bird are tan colored. If the ground color of the bird is green, the bird appears to be a paler greenish brown. It retains the red face. If the ground color is blue, the body color is a soft green-blue with an undertone of brown. It loses the red face, has a creamy white bib, and gets the apricot band across the forehead.

Violet is a factor that adds great beauty to other basic mutations. Violet lovebirds can have a lavender to deep purple rump. In blue lovebirds, the color affects the overall body, making these birds quite striking, especially in direct sunlight.

This factor can be added to most any mutation, but it does not show up in certain birds. For example, if you have a double dark-factored bird, it may darken the feathers too much for the violet to be able to show. Although you cannot see the violet in these birds, this does not mean these are split violet, a common misunderstanding about this factor. In such birds, the violet is simply visually obscured by another color. Quite a bit of variation occurs in the amount of violet showing on the body of violet-factor birds. The main sign that the bird does carry this factor is the lavender or violet rump.

Whitefaced. This is also an additional factor that is added to the basic mutation. A whitefaced bird will have a pure white bib rather than the creamy off-white bib normally seen in blue mutations. The goal for showing in the United States is to eliminate through selective breeding even the pale apricot of the forehead in these birds, although this can be quite difficult to achieve. A whitefaced violet can be an extraordinarily beautiful bird. The pure white face against the bluish violet body is striking.

Sea green, Dutch blue, and whitefaced have created some confusion among lovebird breeders. Without going into the details of genetics, the best way to describe the differences is as follows. Dutch blue and whiteface involve the same allele. For this reason, a bird can carry two Dutch blue genes or two whitefaced genes, or it can carry one Dutch blue gene and one whitefaced gene. If the bird does carry just one of each gene, you have an intermediate color known in the United States as sea green. A

A double-factor violet lovebird is a dramatically beautiful mutation of the peachfaced lovebird. The intensity of the color can vary quite a bit from bird to bird, even within the same clutch.

The whitefaced lovebird has a striking appearance. The goal is to remove as much red psittacin from the crown as possible through selective breeding.

Sea-green and creamino peachfaced lovebirds.

sea-green bird has a more greenish hue to the overall body color, much greener than a Dutch blue. The beak is also two-toned, a sure sign of a sea-green lovebird. If you put two sea-green lovebirds together as a mating pair, you can get some Dutch blues, some sea greens, and some whitefaced blues.

Dark factors. A dark-factored lovebird will have an overall darkening of the main color mutation. This is like the violet factor in that it is a separate element affecting the overall color of the bird. Double dark factors can give you a very dark bird. If the bird's ground color is blue, you will get cobalts with one dark factor and slates or mauves with two dark factors. Slates can sometimes appear to be almost gray in body color, although you can usually still see hints of green in the feathers.

Orangefaced Lovebirds

Orangefaced lovebirds are still peachfaced lovebirds in terms of their species name. The name is used only to describe a genetic factor. Orangefaced lovebirds can be bred into most mutations, although this factor is shown at its best advantage in green birds. The normally reddish face becomes a tangerine color in birds whose ground color is green. This color also looks very striking on green Australian inos and lutinos.

The Eye-Ring Species

Although these species dwell in close geographic proximity in the wild, they remain genetically distinct from one another. The natural barriers in Africa, such as jungles, mountains, and lakes, have kept them separate

In the bird on the left, dark factors deepen the green American cinnamon coloration.

so that hybridization does not happen in their natural setting. This group of lovebirds includes the masked, Fischer's, Nyasa, and black-cheeked species. They are called the eye-ring species because of a pronounced white periophthalmic ring around the eyes. These birds are not sexually dimorphic, meaning distinguishing the sexes simply by visual appearance is generally not easy. The behavior of these four species is somewhat similar. All collect nesting material with the beak rather than tucking it into the feathers the way peachfaced and other lovebird species do. Most of the eye-ring species are threatened in their natural habitat, particularly the black-cheeked and Nyasa lovebirds. For this reason, maintaining pure species lines and not inbreeding the different eye-ring species of lovebirds is essential. In fact, finding pure black-cheeked and Nyasa lovebirds can be difficult. Some attempts have been made, particularly in Germany, to establish pure lines of these birds. In Belgium, top breeders have begun to maintain studbooks for Nyasa lovebirds in an attempt to maintain the purest lines possible.[4]

Breeders have tried to duplicate the red suffusion seen in this peachfaced lovebird, but it seems to be an aberration rather than a mutation.

Masked Lovebirds

Species name: *Agapornis personata personata*

Appearance: The wild-type masked lovebirds have a green body and a blackish brown head and crown that fades to a brownish olive throat and a yellow bib. There is some blue on the tail coverts, the tail is green, and the beak is red. They have a naked white eye ring and gray legs.

Origin: Tanzania, southeast of Lake Victoria; closer to the coast than Fischer's lovebirds. Geography includes inland plateaus, grasslands, and woodlands where baobab trees and acacias are abundant.

Diet: Will eat seed from the ground; considered pests by farmers because they often raid crops, particularly crops of millet and corn.

Sexual dimorphism: No obvious visual differences between the sexes

Breeding: Colony breeders; build nests in the hollows of trees or in holes in buildings. Elaborate nest is built with an internal chamber. Nesting material is carried by the hen in her beak. Lay five to six eggs;

[4]Source: Wessel Louw van der Veen, Belgium.

A yellow-masked lovebird in flight.

body color is a deep blue, and the bird retains the black head and crown. The color reportedly occurred first in the wild. Blue mutations of masked lovebirds are readily available as pets.

Dilute refers to a mutation that results in a dilution of the overall body color through a reduction in melanin throughout the feathers. Both green dilutes and blue dilutes occur as both ground colors can be affected by this genetic factor. Yellow-masked lovebirds are green dilutes that are also split ino, making them heterozygotic birds. Whites are a blue dilute split ino. These birds are similar to their ino counterparts, but the eyes are black rather than red. A white-masked will still show some blue in the body. If you have two white-maskeds in a mating pair, you can get some albino babies; two yellow-maskeds can produce lutino babies.

incubation lasts 23 days; babies fledge in 44 days.

The masked lovebird is a strikingly beautiful bird that can make an extremely tame and affectionate pet when hand-fed. Some parent-raised babies can be tamed if handled early on. Occasionally, the inexperienced will mistake a black-cheeked lovebird for a masked lovebird. Distinguishing between them is important so they are not inadvertently bred together. A general guideline to distinguish these two species is to note the color of the crown of the head. Masked have a full brownish black mask that covers the top of the head; pure black-cheeked lovebirds do not have the dark color on the crown of the head, hence the reasoning behind their common name.

Color Mutations in Masked Lovebirds

One of the most striking mutations is the blue-masked lovebird. The

A normal masked lovebird.

Ino is a lovely mutation in masked lovebirds. This recessive mutation is not sex-linked as it is in peachfaced lovebirds. However, both parents must carry the gene, either visually or as a split, to have visually lutino babies. In green birds, ino is lutino, a bright yellow bird with an orange face and red eyes. In blue birds, it is albino, a pure white bird with red eyes.

Masked lovebird mutations can also be affected by dark factors and violet factors, which cause a change in the feather structure of the bird. A blue-masked with a single dark factor is called a cobalt-masked lovebird. Two dark factors result in a slate-masked lovebird, a bird with a very dark overall body color and white bib and neckline.

Many other mutations have been reportedly bred in the masked lovebirds. However, these are not as common among pet birds.

Fischer's Lovebirds

Species name: *Agapornis personata fischeri*

Appearance: The wild-type has a green body and deep orange forehead, cheeks, and throat. They have a yellow bib and collar, blue and green coverts, green tail, naked white eye ring, red beak, and gray legs.

Origin: Northern Tanzania around Lake Victoria; inland plateaus and grasslands. Sometimes seen at altitudes up to 5,000 feet (1.5 km).

Diet: Seen eating seeds on the ground; sometimes raid crops of millet and corn.

The blue mutation of the black-masked lovebird is commonly called a blue-masked lovebird.

Breeding: The Fischer's have similar breeding habits to the masked lovebirds. Eggs incubate for 23 days, and babies fledge in 38 days.

A black-masked and blue-masked lovebird.

The slate-masked lovebird has blue ground color and double dark factors.

Fischer's lovebirds are smaller than masked lovebirds. These brightly colored beauties also have a slightly louder call than the masked lovebirds. In my aviary where I have both Fischer's and peachfaced lovebirds, the Fischer's calls are easily

A split albino masked lovebird. This bird would need to be paired with another bird split albino or visually albino in order to have albino babies.

distinguished and can be quite high-pitched at times, particularly when excited. Fischer's are separated from masked lovebirds in the wild by dense jungle. Although they do colony breed in the wild, some breeders have found they can be aggressive toward other pairs, more so than masked lovebirds. Therefore, some breeders prefer to pair breed Fischer's lovebirds in separate cages, especially if they are trying to control for specific color mutations.

Hand-fed Fischer's lovebirds make lively pets. Even birds that have not been handled for a while but were formerly quite tame will calm down after some handling. Parent-raised Fischer's can be very skittish around humans.

Color Mutations in Fischer's Lovebirds

Blue Fischer's have a soft blue body, white throat and chest, and some black on the head. This mutation is well established in aviculture, although you do not see it as often among pet Fischer's as you do among pet masked lovebirds.

Dilute in Fischer's works much the same way it does in masked lovebirds. It causes an overall dilution in the body color due to a reduction in melanin. Yellow and white Fischer's are heterozygotic, being split to ino. The yellow Fischer's is split lutino, and the white Fischer's is split albino. If you pair two yellows or two whites together, they can produce lutino and albino babies, respectively.

Ino is a dramatically beautiful mutation in Fischer's lovebirds. The albino is striking with its red eyes. In natural light, you can often see an undertone of blue. The lutino is a bright yellow bird with an orange reddish face, red eyes, and a beak that retains the red.

Fischer's colors can also be influenced by dark factors and violet factors, in much the same way masked lovebirds' colors are. A number of other mutations exist, such as fallow, spangled, and long feather. However, these are not generally available in the pet trade and are kept mainly by experienced breeders and exhibitors of these birds.

A normal Fischer's lovebird.

Black-Cheeked Lovebirds

Species name: *Agapornis personata nigrigens*

Appearance: The wild-type black-cheeked lovebirds have a green body with lighter green underparts. The forehead and front of the crown are dark brown. The nape and back of the crown are light green. Lores, throat, and cheeks are brown-black. The bib is a pale orange-red.

While Fischer's are considered more aggressive than masked lovebirds, they can live peaceably in flights with sufficient space and more nest boxes than there are pairs.

A lutino Fischer's lovebird.

They have a green tail, naked white eye ring, red beak, and grayish brown legs.

Origin: Zambia River valleys, southwest of the area where Nyasa lovebirds are found. They inhabit a very small range in the lowlands, river valleys, and woodlands.

Sexual dimorphism: No obvious visual differences between the sexes.

Breeding: Build elaborate nests; incubation is for 24 days; young fledge in 40 days.

Black-cheeked lovebirds are endangered in the wild. Unfortunately, because of their similarity in appearance to the black-masked lovebird, many uninformed breeders have bred them with masked lovebirds, creating hybrids and reducing the availability of pure lines in aviculture. Due to their low availability, hybridization should be vigorously avoided. The head and mask show distinct differences. A pure black-cheeked lovebird does not have black-brown on the crown.

Black-cheeked lovebirds are not commonly available as pets, although they are occasionally seen. Their behavior is similar to the other eye-ring species. Hand-raised black-cheeked lovebirds will make the best pets.

Color Mutations in Black-Cheeked Lovebirds

The blue mutation is well established in this species. Again, the issue arises of possibly mistaking the blue black-cheeked lovebird with a blue-masked lovebird. This mutation in the black-cheeked lovebird shows an area of white on the upper breast area, which can help one distinguish it from the blue-masked mutation.

The yellow mutation is very rare as of this writing. A few other mutations exist and are most likely due to hybridization with masked or Fischer's lovebirds. These birds are not generally available as pets.

Nyasa Lovebirds

Species name: *Agapornis personata lilianae*

Appearance: They have a green body with lighter green on the underparts and rump. The forehead and throat are a reddish orange that fades to a paler pinkish color on the cheeks, lores, and bib. The tail is green, and they have a naked white eye ring. The beak is red, and the legs are a grayish brown.

Origin: Southern parts of Tanzania and Malawi; area formerly known as Nyasaland and Rhodesia, hence the bird's common name. The area is south of that inhabited by Fischer's and west of that inhabited by masked lovebirds. They live in the river valleys.

Diet: In the wild, they eat seeds, fruits, and berries. They also raid crops of millet.

Sexual dimorphism: No obvious visual differences between the sexes.

Breeding: Build nests in a similar fashion to other eye-ring species; incubation of eggs is for 22 days; babies fledge in 44 days.

As the smallest of the eye-ring species, the Nyasa are somewhat rare in aviculture. These are not birds that are usually kept as pets because their numbers are so low in captivity. They can be raised in colonies as they are known for being a peaceful species.

The black-cheeked lovebird is endangered in the wild.

Color Mutations in Nyasa Lovebirds

The ino mutation is well established in Nyasa lovebirds. The lutino mutation is a bright yellow bird with deep orange head and breast. The eyes are red, as is the beak. A blue

A black-cheeked lovebird in flight.

Nyasa lovebirds in the wild use cavities in trees as nesting places.

mutation has been bred, but these are still quite uncommon.

The Non-Eye-Ring Species

This diverse group of lovebirds is sometimes called the primitive group.

The Nyasa or Lillian's lovebird is rarely seen as a pet.

They have developed differently from the other species already described. The Madagascar is quite different due to its geographic isolation on the island of Madagascar. The red-faced lovebird has unusual nesting habits that have made it a difficult species to establish in aviculture.

Abyssinian Lovebirds

Species: *Agapornis taranta taranta*

Appearance: They have a deep green body, black flight feathers, a strip of black near the edge of the tail feathers, a red beak, and gray legs. Males have a deep red forehead and lores, and a feathered eye ring.

Origin: Ethiopia; they live in the forests and mountain areas up to 9,000 feet (2.7 km).

Diet: In the wild, they eat seeds, berries, juniper berries, and figs. They particularly seem to relish the seeds of fresh figs. In captivity, these birds need more fat in the diet than other lovebird species, which can be supplied with sunflower seeds. Fresh or dried mission figs should also be fed.

Sexual dimorphism: Easy to distinguish sexes once birds have reached around five months of age. Males have red on the lores, forehead, and around the eyes; females have no red on the face.

Breeding: Build nests in the hollows of trees; in captivity, they often like a bare floor in the nest box and hens will spend much time removing any shavings placed in the nest box. In these cases, giving them a wooden insert with a concave area for the eggs, much like the ones given to budgerigars, is best. Lay four or five eggs; incubation lasts for 25 days; young fledge in 50 days.

As the largest of the genus *Agapornis,* Abyssinians are sometimes called black-winged lovebirds. These lovebirds are much more parrotlike in behavior than the other lovebird species. Their chirp is a soft, rough-sounding call that is quite different from the calls of the other lovebird species. Hand-fed males can be quite tame, although hens tend to be shy. In fact, if you inspect the nest box, hens will often cower in the corner. Males are much more curious and forward than hens. They tend to breed best when they are separated into pairs and can hear but not see the other pairs. They are known to be very aggressive, so colony breeding is generally avoided. These birds are also notorious for plucking their mates. In the case of one of my pairs, the male likes to denude the head of his hen completely at breeding time; he lets the feathers grow back after the nesting period is over. In the case of another pair, it is the hen who plucks the male's head.

These birds are still not very common and are rarely seen as pets. However, many breeders are making a concerted effort to increase their numbers in captivity.

Madagascar Lovebirds

Species name: *Agapornis cana cana*

Appearance: Both sexes have a green body that is lighter on the underparts, black coverts, and a

Lutino mutation of the Nyasa lovebird and two normal Nyasa lovebirds.

green tail. The beak and legs are gray. The male has light gray head, neck, and breast area.

Origin: Island of Madagascar off the southeast coast of mainland

Abyssinian lovebirds are sexually dimorphic. The male is on the right.

The Madagascar or gray-headed lovebird is sexually dimorphic. The male is on the left.

Africa. They inhabit the coastal plains and inland foothills. Sometimes seen in desert areas.

Diet: Grass seeds on the ground; raid agricultural crops.

Sexual dimorphism: Males have a gray head, neck, and breast. Females lack this gray coloring, mak-

The female (foreground) red-faced lovebird has a slightly lighter or more orange face than the male.

ing it easy to distinguish between the sexes.

Breeding: Nest in hollows of trees. Nesting material is carried by the hen tucked among her feathers. Generally lay three to five eggs; incubation lasts for 23 days; young fledge in about 44 days.

Madagascar lovebirds are considered to be the most primitive of the genus, having been isolated on the island of Madagascar. One major difference is the size of the beak, which is much smaller proportionally than it is in other lovebird species. They are shy birds in the wild and in captivity. They can be very difficult to breed, which has made it hard to establish them in aviculture. Some breeders have found that offering more than one nest box can encourage breeding. These birds are not seen in the pet trade.

Red-Faced Lovebirds

Species name: *Agapornis pullaria pullaria*

Appearance: Green with some yellow on the underparts. The forehead is red in males, a lighter orangish red in females. The rump is bright blue. Coverts are black, and the tail is green. They have a red beak and gray legs.

Origin: Central and western Central Africa. They inhabit the lowlands, forests, and grasslands of the area.

Diet: In the wild, they feed on young grasses, grass seeds, and fruits such as figs and berries. They sometimes raid agricultural crops, such as millet.

The red-faced lovebird is difficult to breed due to its unusual choice of nesting places, termite mounds.

Appearance: The body is green with a paler green on the head. They have a distinctive black collar around the neck and yellow below the collar. The rump is a grayish blue, flights are black, and the beak is a dark gray.

Origin: Western and Central Africa.

The Swindern's lovebird was inadvertently misspelled when its official name was chosen. It is more correctly called the Swinderen's lovebird and is commonly called the black-collared lovebird. Not much is known about this species. Early attempts to keep these birds in captivity failed miserably. They have never been successfully bred in captivity. One of the issues is the fact that they eat a very specialized diet of fresh fig seeds and occasional millet. They are so rare that one would be hard-pressed to find even a photograph of a living specimen of this species.

Sexual dimorphism: Males have a redder forehead than females.

Breeding: Termite mounds are used as nesting places. Eggs incubate for 22 days, and young fledge in 42 days.

The red-faced lovebird is extremely rare in aviculture. One reason for this is their unusual preference for termite mounds as nesting places. Duplicating this in captivity is difficult, although breeders have found creative ways to do so. They are also considered a more delicate species than the others in the genus.

Swindern's or Swinderen's Lovebirds

Species name: *Agapornis swinderniana swinderniana*

The Swindern's lovebird has never been successfully kept in captivity.

Chapter Eight
Breeding Basics

Preparing a Breeding Program

The popular image of lovebirds is of two birds snuggling together on a branch. Bonded lovebirds can be a joy to watch as they preen each other or wrangle over a toy or bit of food. Because of this, they have become very popular among beginning breeders. However, breeding these birds entails much more than putting two birds together and hanging up a nest box. The most important thing to consider when deciding to breed lovebirds is how much time and energy you have. Breeding birds need to be in top condition; they cannot be on seed-only diets or be forced to live in dirty cages. They must be supplied with a balanced, nutritious diet if they are to raise healthy clutches of babies. You also need to be prepared for emergencies that can arise during the breeding process, from egg binding to parental aggression toward chicks.

A pair of lutino peachfaced lovebirds.

Getting a True Pair of Lovebirds

The most commonly kept lovebird species (peachfaced, Fischer's, masked) are not sexually dimorphic. This means you cannot tell if a lovebird is a male or a female just by looking at it. Some subtle differences occur between males (cocks) and females (hens), but exceptions to these characteristics often arise. Therefore, the best method of determining a lovebird's sex is through DNA testing of blood. A number of labs will send you a free kit and instructions on how to take a sample. The most common method is to clip a toenail a little higher than you normally would and draw the blood into a glass capillary tube. Be sure to have styptic powder on hand to stop the flow of blood when you are done. Unless you are completely sure you can handle the situation should you have difficulties, you should ask your avian veterinarian to take the sample for you. Some bird shops will also take the sample for you and then send it to the lab. This usually doubles your cost, but it is the best option for anyone who is

Bird-Sexing Laboratories

AMR Labs
877-424-1212
http://www.amrlabs.com

Avian Biotech
800-514-9672
http://www.avianbiotech.com/

The National Aviary
412-321-5898
(special rates for lovebirds)
http://www.aviary.org

Some subtle visual and behavioral cues can indicate the sex. However, relying on these could delay results in your breeding program.

Exceptions to all these general characteristics do occur. I have seen males who are quite expert at tucking and carrying nesting material. However, they are usually better at stealing the nesting material from the hen's wings. Of course, if a bird lays an egg, you know it is a hen. However, that does not mean its mate is male. When two birds are hens is often clear because 10 to 12 eggs will be in the nest box rather than the usual six or seven.

not confident about being able to obtain the blood sample safely.

Another method used to determine sex is surgical sexing. This is a more invasive procedure and must be done by a qualified avian veterinarian. This method is generally unnecessary for lovebirds now that DNA sexing techniques are more than 99 percent reliable when the tests are performed by a qualified laboratory.

Picking Healthy Stock

The quality of your initial breeding stock will have a long-term impact on the quality of your breeding program. So be sure you choose healthy, robust birds from the beginning. This

Hens
• Wider stance on the perch
• Often a bit larger than males
• Pelvic space is wider
• Pelvic bones move when carefully touched with a finger
• Tuck nesting material under the wings
• Sit in the nesting box most of the time
• More aggressive in protecting territory; likely to bite

Males
• Regurgitate for the hens
• Tucked nesting material tends to fall from wings
• Sit outside the nesting box most of the time
• Not as likely to attack to protect territory
• Rub the perch or cage bars as if mating
• Sit outside box during day

Compatible birds will sit close together on the perch. However, this does not guarantee that a pair is male and female.

might mean selecting more expensive birds and buying fewer at first. This is a much better idea than buying large groups of average birds at a low cost. Often, price does reflect the quality of care that birds receive. A breeder who feeds a varied, quality diet and does not overcrowd his or her aviaries has higher expenses than one who has a few huge flights filled with birds who are fed just seeds and water.

Breeders who pair breed and keep good records of breeding lines and genetics (for example, splits) have much higher expenses than those who aviary breed and do not specifically arrange pairings of certain birds.

You can expect to pay more if you get your bird from such breeders, but you will often get better background information about your birds.

A bird should be in good feather. Young birds tend to have diluted colors, but you can still see if the feathers have a nice sheen to them. Turn the bird over onto its back and feel along either side of the bird's keel bone (the bone that basically divides the bird in half) to make sure it is not underweight. A nice amount of flesh should be on either side of the bone. Also, avoid birds who have stained vents. Diarrhea could be a sign of bacterial infection or other illnesses. Bright eyes and clean nares (nose area) are also important signs. Avoid birds who have poor feathering and appear to be plucking themselves. There is a rising problem of lovebirds who pluck themselves (feather mutilation), and this can become an ongoing, intractable problem in an aviary. Plucking on the back of the head is usually done by other, more aggressive birds in a flight or cage or by a mate during the breeding season and does not generally impact potential breeding success. However, plucking of leg feathers, chest feathers, and other areas a bird can reach on itself can possibly be the sign of a bird that has a condition sometimes referred to as lovebird pyoderma. Read more about this in Chapter 4, "Avian Health."

These baby peachfaced lovebirds are close to fledging and will soon venture from the nest box.

Putting Together a New Pair

One of the biggest mistakes new breeders make is to put a new bird in with an established bird. Putting a new male into a hen's established territory can be disastrous. Lovebirds are extremely territorial and will fight, even kill, a bird who treads in their space. Lovebirds should be introduced in a divided cage or in two cages side-by-side at first. When they start to sit on the end of the perch closest to each other, you can then try introducing them to each other in a single cage.

Not all lovebirds are compatible. While they do not have to experience love at first sight, if one of the birds you are trying to pair shows aggression toward its intended mate, you have to be very cautious. Hens tend to be the more aggressive one when they do not like the mate you have chosen. They will sometimes prevent the male from eating and will bite feet, legs, and the back of the neck. Bites on the back of the neck can be fatal. So watch carefully, and separate birds immediately if this type of aggression is occurring.

Cages and Nest Boxes

There are two ways to breed lovebirds: in large groups in flights or by individual pairs in separate breeding cages. If you want to control the color mutations and genetic lines, the latter method is preferable. Keeping the peace among lovebirds is also much easier when they have separate cages. Despite their name, lovebirds can be rather aggressive toward other birds. You can remove pairs from flight cages at breeding time and place them into smaller cages more suitable for breeding. An ideal breeder cage should be at least 24 inches by 18 inches by 18 inches (60 cm by 45 cm by 45 cm). The birds should be able to beat their wings without hitting the cage sides or perches. They should be able to climb and play for exercise.

Many people think that supplying toys and the like will distract birds from mating. I do not find this to be true. Birds with an interesting and stimulating environment are happier and hence more likely to make good parents. Do not forget that lovebirds are very playful, clownish creatures, and they need an appropriate stage for their antics.

The nest box is your next consideration. While many people use a large parakeet or cockatiel box, I usually get the best results with English budgie nesting boxes. These open on one end via a sliding, two-part door. They have a little raised platform at the entrance and a lower area for the hen to nest. These are nice because the hen can have company while nesting without being crowded. The cock will sit on the perch over the raised platform or will sleep directly on the raised platform. This also decreases the chances of eggs being cracked if there is ever a panicked rush into the nest box. The birds dive onto the raised platform first and then move down to the lower nesting area.

Make sure the sliding doors are not swollen due to moisture. This makes inspecting the eggs difficult. Your hens will feel less agitated if you do not have to wiggle and force the door every time you want to check on them. If the doors are very tight in the grooves, remove them, file or sand down the edges a bit, then put them back in and test for easy sliding.

If you hang the nest box on the outside of the cage and then use wire clippers to cut a hole in the cage bars for the nest box entrance, you will be able to check on the hen and babies more easily. Make sure you file down any sharp points on the cut wire.

A lutino peachfaced hen peers out from her nest box.

Blue-masked baby lovebirds in the nest box.

Nesting Material

A basic substrate of pine shavings or commercially available paper nesting material such as CareFresh[5] should be put into the box to give it a soft bottom. A couple of inches will give the hen a good base for her nest and prevent leg problems with your chicks (see "Preventing Splay-Legged Babies," page 116). Make sure any material you use is labeled safe for use with birds. Cedar can be toxic to birds. Also, do not use corncob bedding or walnut shells. First, they are very uncomfortable, and second, they are dangerous if ingested. Corncob can swell in a baby's crop and can also serve as a breeding ground for *Aspergillus*

species. Walnut shells have been known to do damage to the digestive system because of their sharp edges. These items should not be used as cage liner either since parents may ingest them and feed them to their babies. Some species will balk at being given nesting material. Abyssinian lovebirds will push the material aside until they can find the flat wooden floor. You can arrange the material so that it creates a ring around this exposed area, which prevents eggs from rolling around in the nest box.

Humidity is very important for the successful hatching of lovebird eggs. In areas where the weather is extremely dry, many lovebird breeders supply wetted palm fronds as nesting material. Lovebirds will shred the long fronds and stuff them under their wings until they look like little pin cushions. They then take them into the nest box and proceed to build their nests. I have also used shredded white paper towels, eucalyptus, and dried grasses. Lovebirds will use their own lost feathers for the nest too. Supply new nesting material even after the eggs are laid, as this keeps the nest fresher and keeps up the appropriate humidity level (the wetted fronds do this). You can also get nesting material at pet supply stores, but you really do not need to spend money on these. Do not give leaves of any poisonous plants or plants that have been treated with insecticides. To control this, I use palm trees from my yard. If you do not live in a southern clime,

[5]CareFresh, Absorption Corporation, Bellingham, WA 98225. *http://www.carefresh.ca*

this could be difficult. However, you can investigate an appropriate, non-poisonous substitute in your geographic area. In particularly dry areas, spritzing the birds with water as hatching time nears can help you maintain proper humidity levels. Be careful not to wet the wooden nest box because this could encourage the growth of mold.

Nutrition for Breeding Birds and Their Young

Nutrition is what ultimately determines the health and quality of your babies once you have chosen healthy, genetically diverse stock for breeding pairs. Many companies make a pelleted diet specifically intended for breeding birds. These pellets are higher in protein than are maintenance pellets. However, do not rely solely on these for nutrition. Supply seeds, vegetables, and grains as well. Occasionally, pieces of fruit are fine, but they are not a substitute for vegetables. The simplest way to give lovebirds excellent green nutrition is by feeding fresh wheatgrass. Most lovebirds will take to it quickly. It is easy to feed, does not spoil, and guarantees a wide spectrum of vitamins and minerals. Sprouted seeds are also an excellent source of high-quality nutrition. However, they must be served fresh or after no more than three days in the refrigerator due to the risk of bacterial growth. Washing sprouts in a solution of water and either bleach (not bleach with lye; make it a 50:1 dilution of water to bleach) or grapefruit seed extract then rinsing thoroughly can reduce the risk of bacterial contamination. Remember that fresh foods indicate spring to birds, much in the same way that longer sunlight hours do. Cooked grains such as quinoa and oat groats are relished by breeding birds.

Eggs in the Nest Box

Hens lay between five and seven eggs usually. First-time mothers may lay fewer eggs. They lay them approximately every other day. Do not be concerned if the hen does not sit tight on the eggs at first. Some hens will not settle in full-time to incubate the eggs until they have laid the third one. After that, you will not see her out of the nest box very

Eggs are less likely to be broken by the hen if they sit on soft nesting material.

often. The male will help feed her by regurgitating. She will come out on occasion for short visits to the water or food dish or to relieve herself. You may notice that her poops are much larger and softer during this period.

You can determine whether eggs are fertile approximately five days after the hen begins sitting tight. The best point at which to check is five days after incubation has begun, which is usually five days after the third egg is laid. A special device called a candler is used to do this. You should get one of these inexpensive tools because they have a special protective hood that prevents you from chipping the egg or overheating it. A fertile egg first shows little red veins. As the chick develops, the veins are no longer visible and the egg becomes darker where the body is developing. Infertile eggs, known as clear, have a pale yellow appearance with no dark formations.

Approximately 23 days after an egg is laid, the chick should being to pip. A chick can take up to 24 hours to work its way fully out of the shell. I have rarely found it necessary to help a lovebird chick hatch. Some species, such as Abyssinians, can take even longer to extricate themselves from the egg. Overly nervous breeders often interfere with this process, afraid the chick is taking too long to hatch. This is often a mistake and can actually harm the chick more than it helps. If for some reason you feel it is necessary to help the chick, the egg must be removed slowly, a little bit every hour rather than all at once. The chick should always be left attached to the soft material inside the egg. This egg sac contains essential nutrition that the chick will absorb. If you remove this material, the chick will die. In most cases, helping the chick from the egg is a mistake. If done improperly, it will result in the death of the chick. If you continually have problems with chicks unable to extricate themselves from the shell on their own, you may have an aviary management issue, such as too much calcium in the diet, causing excessive hardness of the shell.

Preventing Egg Binding

Egg binding and a more serious complication, egg peritonitis, can be deadly to a hen. This occurs when an egg is too soft or too large for the hen to pass. The egg is essentially stuck inside her. An egg-bound hen will look sick, often sitting puffed up on the floor of the cage. If you turn over such a hen, you will see a very swollen vent. This is an emergency situation. Get the hen warm immediately. If you do not have a professional brooder, keep a plastic reptile container and heating pad on hand at all times in case this situation arises. Getting an egg-bound bird to an avian veterinarian within 12 to 24 hours is important if you want the bird to survive. If the egg breaks inside her, she will be at risk for peritonitis. Sometimes a course of antibiotics will help in these cases, but often the bird will not survive or will be incapable of breeding in the future. The risk of egg binding increases when birds are not given a rest between clutches, hens are not given sufficient calcium (cuttlebone), or hens are bred too young (under one year of age).

Infertile Eggs

A number of conditions can cause infertile eggs. Often, a young breeding pair just does not quite get it right the first time around. Do not give up. Usually, they are more successful the second time around. Give them a couple of weeks of rest, and put the nest box back up to try again.

Bacterial infections can result in infertility, especially if left untreated. Low-grade infections might not be immediately apparent. A veterinary checkup that includes a fecal smear and cloacal swab will determine if your birds have an underlying bacterial problem that could be causing infertility.

Loose perches can lead to infertile eggs. If the perch is loose the male cannot get good contact with the female. They might do the dance, but it will be to no avail. Give each perch a little shake to see if it is stable enough.

Why Fertile Eggs Don't Hatch

Poor nutrition, a hen letting eggs get cold during brooding, bacterial infections, not enough humidity, and genetic defects are all possible causes for dead-in-shell chicks. Determining why some eggs just do not hatch is not always easy. In my experience, sometimes one or two eggs simply do not hatch, often the last one or two laid.

Obviously, if a large number of eggs are not hatching, you should be concerned. Break open the long-overdue eggs to see the level of development the chick achieved. If the chick has only rudimentary development, the hen may have let the eggs get cold at that point during incubation. If you noticed the hen was outside the nest box for considerable periods of time during the brooding process, this may be the problem.

Peachfaced eggs and the first hatch.

Genetic defects can result in dead chicks in the shell. This cause is difficult to confirm. If a pair continues to have this problem, separating and pairing them with new mates to see if this changes anything may be best. Sometimes a pair could be a poor genetic match, and pairing with new mates is your best bet. Before doing this, however, an avian veterinarian should rule out health problems. One of the most cited problems that can be considered genetic in origin occurs when you breed two red-eyed parents (ino mutations). Many breeders recommend that you not put two red-eyed birds together. This can sometimes result in weak chicks that do not thrive, blindness, and other genetic problems. For example, breeding a lutino hen with a male that is split lutino is best. Genetic problems can also be due to inadvertent breeding of too closely related birds. This is why record keeping is very important (see next page).

If the chicks are fully formed, the problem could be with hatching itself. Low humidity or too-hard shells due to overuse of calcium in the diet can be causes. A cuttlebone is sufficient for calcium, so do not also add calcium supplements to water and food. If you live in a dry climate, you can use the wetted palm fronds (see page 112) or mist the cage once a day to supply moisture. Do not soak the nest box because this can cause mold to grow. If you mist the father, he will often go into the nest box and bring the moisture with him.

Preventing Splay-Legged Babies

You know it when you see it. The legs are spread straight out, and the chick is unable to get a grip and sit up with its legs properly underneath its body. Splay legs can be very traumatic for the novice breeder. The best way to deal with this is to prevent it. Even the best nest builders should be given a basic substrate for the nest box (see page 112). Put about 2 to 3 inches (5 to 8 cm) into the nest box, then give the hen other nest-building materials. She will build her nest on top of the substrate. This prevents the chicks from ending up on the bottom of a nest box on a slippery wooden floor where they cannot get a proper grip. It also cushions them if they have an overzealous mother who sits very tightly on them. If you have already got chicks in the nest and realize they are hitting the wooden floor, remove the chicks, remove the nest built by the mother (try to keep it basically intact), add 2 to 3 inches (5 to 8 cm) of safe nesting material, place the mother's nest on top of the substrate, and then put the chicks back into the box.

If you have a baby with splay legs, the best way to treat it is to double band the legs and use dental floss to tie the legs together in the proper position under the body. Place the baby into a cup with soft cushioning (unscented tissues are good) to help it rest comfortably. This entails pulling the baby from the nest and hand-feeding it separately from other chicks, as the string between the legs can strangle other chicks in the nest. If you are having difficulty, take the baby to the veterinarian immediately. You do not want to let this go, as these birds are often severely crippled and will need special caging and extra help all their lives. Another method uses a makeup sponge to keep the legs together. Catching this problem early on is important. It can usually be corrected if the bird is put in the hobble by the time it is 21 days old. Leave the hobble on for at least one week, longer if the bird is over 14 days old, then check to see if it is corrected. For either method, you will most likely need to replace the hobble a couple of times because it will stretch or become loosened.

Baby Fischer's lovebirds on appropriate bedding.

Keeping Records

Keeping good breeding records is important for a number of reasons. The most important is to prevent inbreeding down the road. Someone may buy some birds from you one year, then buy more a few years later to add to their breeding collection. You want to be able to tell them which of these new birds is related to the birds they bought the previous year.

Keeping track of genetics is also important. Many colors can be splits (see the color genetics information under each species for more about this). You need to be able to tell buy-ers that a male bird might be split to American cinnamon or lutino since this will determine what color babies they get. Most serious breeders do not like to be surprised by a mutation, especially when they are working to achieve certain color lines.

The best way to keep good records is to band your birds. Traceable bands can be ordered from the African Lovebird Society *(http://www.africanlovebirdsociety.com)*. You do need to become a member to be eligible to receive these bands. These will have your initials, the hatch year, and a unique number to identify the birds. When you band a bird, you write down the number alongside its date of birth. Make a note of its parents' colors and names/band numbers.

This sort of record keeping becomes more important as the

Eye-ring lovebirds often build elaborate cave-like nests. These are young masked lovebirds.

years pass. In lines where you have fourth- and fifth-generation babies, knowing who is related to whom is very important to avoid inbreeding. Remembering this once you have a large collection of birds can become impossible. Written records are the only guarantee you have that you are matching up appropriate birds for future stock.

Hatching Eggs

The first few days after the eggs begin hatching can be nerve-racking for beginners. Resist the temptation to check on the babies too often, but do make sure they are being properly fed by the parents. Your job is to make this stressful job as easy on the parents as possible. The male

has to eat his food, regurgitate it for the hen, who in turn regurgitates the food for the babies. This involves enormous amounts of energy, and you might notice the male parent getting a little on the thin side. Later on, the male will help feed the babies himself rather than using the female as a go-between.

The best way to ease the stress on the parents is to supply a wide variety of easy-to-digest foods on a regular basis. I always give parents more meals than other lovebirds. They need their water replaced more often; you will notice it gets dirtier much faster. They will prefer softer, hence fresh, foods that cannot be left in the cage for more than a few hours. For people working nine-to-five jobs, this can be difficult. Give fresh foods as soon as you get up in the morning, then just before you leave for work remove anything that can spoil. Leave in the cage millet, dried egg food (a powdery yellow food found at most avian supply stores) or Quiko, pellets, vegetables that do not spoil easily such as wheatgrass or raw broccoli florets, and a good seed mix. Give them fresh food again when you arrive home, and take it out after an hour or so.

Make sure the parents also have cuttlebone and plenty of water. Give them two bowls of water during this period. They will usually make a mess of one right away but will often leave one unsoiled for a few hours. With particularly messy parents you may have to change the water three times a day. Many like to make soup with their pellets since this creates a very easy-to-feed mush.

You will notice the babies are on their backs for the first few days. This is completely normal. Lovebirds always feed their babies on their backs. If for some reason you are forced to pull lovebird babies that are this young, you will have to do the same. Feeding one-day-old babies is extremely difficult and time-consuming. It should not be attempted by a beginner. If you are forced to do this because the mother is ignoring the babies or attacking them, you should get help from an experienced hand-feeder. You will have to feed these babies every 15 minutes to half an hour if they are only a few days old. This can test the patience of most anyone. Waiting until chicks are at least a week old to pull them for hand-feeding is best.

Parent Aggression Toward Chicks

Lovebirds generally make excellent parents. However, on occasion you will have either a hen or cock who will show aggression toward babies. This can range from plucking their feathers to maiming or killing them. When you begin a breeding program, you should always be prepared to pull chicks should the parents show dangerous aggression toward their young. Even if you did

not intend to hand-feed the babies, you need to have the brooder, hand-feeding formula, thermometer, and syringes on hand for emergencies. You need to learn the basics of hand-feeding well before such an emergency arises. You do not want to have to find someone to give you instruction when six babies with empty crops are staring up at you.

Hand-feeding

If you intend your babies to be pets, hand-feeding them is best. Different breeders like to pull their babies at various ages. Generally, babies at 10 to 14 days of age will immediately take to the syringe and readily eat the warm formula. Some breeders will wait as long as three weeks to pull chicks for hand-feeding, but sometimes these birds can be a little resistant to the syringe at first.

Place the chicks into a brooder. This can be made using a plastic reptile container filled with some nesting material. Placing plain paper towels on top of the soft nesting material can help for easier cleaning at each feeding. You can put a heating pad under the container. Keep it on low or medium, and check to make sure the babies are not panting from too much heat. Also, if you place the pad under only one-half of the container, the babies can move away from the heat source if they find it too warm. By 21 days, the lovebirds have a good amount of feathering and are old enough to create warmth by cuddling with each other. Do not leave dirty, soiled liners in the brooder since baby birds are very susceptible to bacterial infections, and poops equal bacteria. Also, as they get older, curious chicks will eat their own poops. Use the extra large brooder so the babies can grow into it. One side is for cuddling, one side is for food bowls. You can put a stand-alone perch into the brooder when the babies are about four weeks old. They can be transferred to a cage at six weeks of age.

Be properly trained before attempting hand-feeding. I found a local bird store where they were willing to let me watch and learn. Once I had done this for a while, I took home my own bird to feed. I would bring the bird back in so the store employees could check his weight every other day until we were sure I was on the right track. Hand-feeding is not an exact science. You will find each bird is very different. Some are easy to feed, some are fussy and take longer to fill with formula. Some birds wean quickly; some take a few weeks longer. If you want healthy birds that are not neurotic about food, you will learn from them rather than follow a rigid system. You have to be very careful that a bird is getting enough formula and that no formula is getting into the bird's lungs. This is called aspiration and can be fatal. It can cause immediate asphyxiation or a slower death due to pneumonia.

Lovebirds pulled from the nest at 14 days of age require around five feedings a day at first. This may vary depending how how thick your formula is and how quickly the bird's crop empties. Hand-rearing formula can be found at most pet stores. The formula should be between 103 and 105°F (39 and 41°C). If you are getting refusals, check the temperature again because the formula may have cooled down too much. Get a quality digital thermometer to test the temperature. If the formula is too cold, lovebirds will balk at being fed. If it is too hot, you can burn the crop. All it takes is one time with too-hot formula to injure your bird critically by burning its crop.

Do not use a microwave oven to heat your formula. Doing so can cause hot spots in the formula that could burn the bird's crop. You must stir formula thoroughly before testing the temperature.

When you begin feeding a new clutch, the formula should be rather thin. Generally, the companies that make formulas give good specifications as to ratios between water and powder. Just as a general formula, start with a thin mixture then progress to a mixture with a pea-soup texture over the next two weeks.

O-ring syringes work best and are the easiest to plunge at the right rate. You do not want to plunge so quickly that you choke the bird. You also do not want to plunge so slowly that you frustrate the bird and it swallows too much air. If you stir the formula with the plunger part of the syringe before putting the syringe together, it will slide more smoothly.

Do not force the formula; let the baby set the rhythm. They pump as they eat, and you should slowly use this pumping to determine how quickly you push down on the plunger of the syringe. If the bird stops, wait until it is ready for a bit more. Generally, these pauses last only a second or so. This is something you get better at the more you hand-feed.

You do not need to force the food into the crop. This method, often called *power feeding,* is not the best way to feed a baby. Let it taste the food in its mouth. This is the beginning of eating for a baby, and you are not doing it a service by forcing the formula into its crop.

Clean your syringes thoroughly between feedings. Normal household bleach diluted in water (1:32) is a good disinfectant. However, be sure to rinse the syringe and plunge clean water through it until it is completely clean. Antibacterial dishwashing soap can also be used. Use hot water to clean and rinse your syringes.

Begin to supply your birds with a variety of foods starting around five to six weeks of age. The best eaters are the ones exposed to various foods at an early age. Sunflower sprouts, cereal, and crumbled pellets are good for starters. A bird usually needs a few days to catch on. Change the types of food you give so the bird will get used to seeing new, strange items. This results in a bird who is willing to try new foods right through adulthood. Cooked vegetables such as carrots, corn, peas, and broccoli; bits of whole-wheat bread and cooked grains; and some seed should be given. You do not have to worry about teaching your bird to like seed as this comes naturally. It needs to be exposed to the vegetables and other foods early on so it will eat a well-balanced diet as a juvenile and adult.

Weaning

In the wild, lovebirds fledge, or leave the nest, at around six weeks of age. However, parents continue to feed them for a couple of weeks after fledging. The babies will be able to eat on their own, but these supplemental feedings help them through the transition. This is true of most parrot species.

The concept of abundance weaning[6] has recently gained popularity. While tracking the lives of birds once a breeder sells them can be diffiicult, many personal anecdotes from breeders give credence to the idea that abundance weaning leads to more secure, less neurotic birds who will eat a wider variety of foods.

Abundance weaning simply means you let the bird decide when it is done being hand-fed. You never starve the bird to get it to eat. In fact, birds are more likely to pick at new foods if they have had their appetite stimulated by a shot of formula.

---

[6]Phoebe Greene Linden, page 13.

This type of hybrid lovebird, a cross between a peachfaced and masked lovebird, is strongly discouraged by aviculturists.

My lovebirds start to get a little annoyed by the syringe at five or six weeks of age. They still want the food but do not want to be totally filled with formula. They balk if you try to give them the usual size feeding. Do not force the issue. Let them have their taste, then supply them with as wide a variety of foods as possible.

Lovebirds do tend to thin down quite a bit during the weaning process. Pay careful attention to this as you do not want the bird to get too thin. Lovebirds are just not big pigs when they wean the way budgies are. Budgies will stuff themselves with millet until their crops are so big they can barely stand up. Lovebirds tend to eat a little all day long rather than pig out. The exception is during parenting, when lovebird pairs with babies will tend to have very full crops all the time to be prepared to regurgitate food for screaming babies.

Your bird is weaned when it no longer begs/cries for foods and appears to be eating normally. Nothing is wrong with offering a little formula just to be sure. However, if your bird has been going four days on just a tad of formula, you can be pretty sure it is weaned. Going a little longer with hand-feeding is always better than to wean too quickly. Hand-fed babies do tend to take longer to wean than parent-raised birds. Weaning age can range from seven to nine weeks generally. Sometimes the runt of the litter will take even longer.

Do not send your babies to their new homes right away. Waiting three or four more days to be sure the bird is fully weaned is better. You will know pretty quickly if the bird's appearance or vitality has subtly changed. A new owner might not notice the subtle signs that you would notice. These few extra days can also prevent regression, a phenomenon that can occur with birds weaned a bit too quickly or just insecure birds looking for mama. This is when the bird wants to hand-feed again after being off formula for a few days. It can sometimes occur when a bird goes through the stress of being in a strange, new home.

Selling Unweaned Babies

This practice can be deadly. Be absolutely sure that you do not sell an unweaned baby to someone who either you have not trained yourself to hand-feed or who does not have proven experience raising a baby through weaning. Crop burning, malnutrition, and aspirated formula are just some of the problems that can arise when an inexperienced person tries to hand-feed a baby. If you are considering buying an unweaned baby, do not take this responsibility lightly. It is a myth that you have to hand-feed a baby parrot for it to bond to you.

Socializing

The closer the bird is to weaning, the more important it is that you handle the bird regularly to avoid the phenomenon of babies going wild. Even picking up babies for a minute or two of snuggling between feedings will help them feel more confident and comfortable with human hands.

Once the bird weans, it can easily go wild if it is not handled daily. This is why so many people who buy lovebirds in pet shops end up being disappointed with their birds. They are told the babies were hand-fed and just need some handling to tame them again. However, if a bird has totally reverted to its wild nature, calming it down again can be all but impossible. This reversion can happen rather quickly, especially if the bird was not handled much during the hand-feeding process. Once a bird has reached about five to six months of age, it does not have to be handled as much to retain its tameness. Birds that are interacted with on a daily basis during the first five months of life will often remain tame even after being placed into a breeding situation, although hens will usually become aggressive once a nest box has been put up.

Rest for Parents

Pairs should be allowed to rest between clutches. Sometimes if a pair has only a few chicks, it can be allowed to double-clutch (immediately go back to nest) after you have pulled for hand-feeding. However, usually the birds will need a couple of months of rest. Pairs should be allowed to produce only three clutches a year. The nest box should be removed to make sure the birds do not go back to nest too soon.

Breeding and raising lovebirds is a wonderful hobby or profession. However, being fully prepared for any contingency that could arise during the breeding season is important. Picking quality birds, feeding a nutritious diet, and preparing for emergencies will help assure that the experience will be a rewarding and joyous one.

Chapter Nine

The Genetics of Color

How Colors Work

This chapter is not intended for those who already have some knowledge of the principles of inheritance. This is basically a primer for those who have never ventured into the field of genetics. The purpose is to give the pet owner and the beginning breeder some knowledge about why their bird is the color it is. The information focuses on the most commonly kept species: peach-faced, masked, and Fischer's lovebirds. First, understanding some basic elements that make up the feathers of parrots is important. Then the text will define how these colors and factors are inherited in the three species.

Ground color: This term describes the basic color of the bird. Although often called green series and blue series, these two groups can also be affected by a number of other changes in the feather, thereby creating such colors as albino, lutino, and American cinnamon, which are

There is not a true blue mutation of the peachfaced lovebird, hence the more greenish blue coloration seen in this color variety.

visually unique depending on the ground color of the bird. For example, you can can have blue American cinnamons as well as green American cinnamons.

The Tyndall effect: A lovebird cannot truly be said to be green or blue in the sense that it has pigments of those colors in its feathers. Rather, the effect of blue light reflecting off the feather creates the illusion of these colors.

Melanin: Melanin pigments are black and brown protein granules in the feather structure. The size and number of these granules affects the color of the bird by making the colors appear lighter or darker. The location and size of these granules affects the overall ground color of the bird.

Psittacin pigment: Although sometimes called carotenoids, these are the red and yellow pigments present in feathers. The term carotenoid may be familiar to you. It is what gives carrots, squash, and other yellow, red, and orange vegetables their color.

The overall visual color of the bird (its phenotype) is determined by three things:

These normal and pied lovebirds both have green ground color.

1. The amount and location of melanin.

2. The amount of red and/or yellow psittacin pigment.

3. The structure of what is called the cloudy layer of the feather, which is the area that surrounds the melanin granules.

If you have a lovebird with yellow and red psittacin, no change in the melanin, and add the effect of light scattering, you see the wild-type peachfaced lovebird with a green body and red face.

Color Mutations

The following will discuss only the most common categories of color varieties in lovebirds.

Blue: No true blue color exists in peachfaced lovebirds. It is better described as par-blue, marine, or green-blue. You may have heard the term Dutch blue used as well. To achieve true blue, you need a complete absence of red and yellow psittacin. How the light scatters or reflects from such feathers gives the appearance of blue. In peachfaced lovebirds there is only a partial reduction in yellow and red psittacin. True blue mutations occur in Fischer's and masked lovebirds.

Dilute: This is exactly what it sounds like: a dilution of color. For example, a blue dilute is a color somewhere between blue and white. There is a slight reduction in melanin but not enough to produce a completely white bird.

Pied: In a pied peachfaced lovebird there are areas in the feather structure where melanin is absent and some where it is reduced. These areas will show as variegated yellows, blues, and greens. You also see a reduction in red psittacin in these birds, so they do not have the typical red face of the wild-type peachfaced lovebird.

Ino: Rather than jump right to the commonly used terms of lutino, creamino, and albino, first understanding the concept behind the ino mutation is best. Ino birds have no melanin, even in the eyes. The eyes appear to be red or ruby in these birds. If you have a peachfaced lovebird whose ground color is green, ino expresses itself as lutino, a bright yellow bird with a lighter red face and red eyes. If you have a peachfaced lovebird whose ground color is blue, it will express itself as creamino, a red-eyed, pale yellow bird due to the presence of some yellow psittacin. In a blue Fischer's or masked lovebird, it will express itself as albino because these are true blue mutations and there is a complete absence of psittacin.

Australian cinnamon: This is not actually a true cinnamon but, rather, an ino mutation. Many people prefer the term *Australian ino* for this bird. Slightly more melanin occurs in the Australian cinnamon than in the lutino. Therefore, the eyes appear ruby during the first few weeks of life but darken to a brownish shade as the bird matures. However, because the mechanism behind this mutation is similar to that behind the lutino, it can be more accurately described as an ino color. This mutation in peachfaced lovebirds creates a unique situation. A male peachfaced lovebird can essentially carry the genetic makeup for both lutino and Australian cinnamon. These birds are called split cinnamoninos.

Cinnamon: True cinnamon, called American cinnamon in peachfaced lovebirds, is due to black melanin being replaced by brown melanin, giving the bird a more cinnamon or light brown appearance. The actual appearance of the bird depends on whether the ground color is blue or green.

Dark factors: This is a separate element that affects the bird's overall color by darkening it. Dark factors are not a color in and of themselves but, rather, are due to a change in the structure of the feather barb, affecting how it reflects light. A single dark factor will deepen the ground color of the bird, creating a medium green or medium blue. Double dark factors result in the total loss of the reflection of blue light, producing olive (greens) and slate (blues).

Violet factor: The violet factor works in a similar fashion to the dark factors. It is also due to a change in the feather structure. This color can be obscured in a bird with double dark factors. However, it can deepen to a beautiful deep purple when a single dark factor is present.

Whitefaced: This change in the face and bib of the peachfaced lovebird is due to a further reduction of psittacin in a bird with blue (par-blue) ground color. Whitefaced and what is traditionally called Dutch blue (or simply blue) genes exist on the same allele. You can have two Dutch blue genes to have a Dutch blue bird or two whitefaced genes to have a whitefaced bird. If you have one Dutch blue and one whitefaced gene, you have a seagreen bird.

Sea green: Sea green is best described as somewhere between blue and green, intermediate to whitefaced. The overall body color is more green than in the blues. Many times the belly is much lighter green. The beak is two-toned. In terms of being an intermediate factor to whitefaced, if you have two sea-green lovebirds together, some of their young may be whitefaced. You increase the odds of getting white-faced babies by having one white-faced parent in the pair.

Genetic Terminology

These are some of the more common terms you will hear when discussing the colors of parrots. However, these only scratch the surface.

Split: When a bird is said to be split to a certain color, the bird carries the color genetically but does not express it visually. It can pass this color to its young, depending on the mode of inheritance of the particular color. If you have two green birds split blue, they both look green but can have blue progeny. This gets more complicated when you have birds split for sex-linked or sex-linked recessive colors. Splits are commonly written as the visual color, followed by a slash, then the split color. For example, green/blue denotes a visually green bird split blue. This convention will be used throughout this chapter. Because of splits, two lovebirds can be the same phenotype (they look the same) but be different genotypes (they carry different genetic information). This is why people are sometimes surprised by a baby in their clutches of peachfaced lovebirds. If you have two green lovebirds and a lutino hatches in a clutch, you can be sure this baby is a hen because only a male can be split lutino and he can pass it only to his daughters.

Sex-linked: Colors that are sex-linked can be passed from the parent of one sex to babies of the opposite sex either as a split (hens to male babies) or as a visual color (cocks to female babies). To get babies of both sexes in the sex-linked color, both parents must carry the color, either visually or as a split. Only males can be split to a sex-linked color. Hens either show the color visually or do not carry it.

Dominant: You often hear about a color being dominant. Maybe you are a beginning breeder who put together a green hen and blue cock. You got all green babies and cannot figure out why you did not get any blue babies. The reason is that green is a dominant color. Both par-

The many mutations of eye-ring lovebirds create a beautiful rainbow of color.

ents must be blue, either visually or as a split, for the babies to express blue visually. Babies from the pair where only one parent is blue will be visually green, split blue. If you have two green parents split blue, you will get some visually blue babies.

Autosomal dominant: Genetic inheritance of an autosomal dominant trait depends on whether one or both parents carry the mutation. Pied is an example of an autosomal dominant mutation. If you have one green parent and one pied parent, some or all of the babies will be pied. If you have two pied parents, all babies will be pied.

Autosomal incomplete dominance: Both parents must show the color for babies to show it. However, the degree of the effect will vary depending on its expression in the parents. Violet factor is a good

example of this. Violet can look very different in babies than in their parents. The appearance of both parents has an impact on the appearance of progeny. A difference in appearance also occurs if both parents carry the violet factor and if either or both carry single or double violet factors. A bird cannot be split to a violet factor. It either shows this color or does not carry it. However, double dark factors can obscure violet factors, which has led to the misconception that birds can be split violet.

Autosomal complete dominance: There will be no difference in appearance whether single or double factor. However, the number of factors influences the number of young inheriting the factor by increasing the percentages of babies showing this variety.

Inheritance of Lutino in Peachfaced Lovebirds*

Mother	Father	Female Babies	Male Babies
Green	Green/Lutino	Green Lutino	Green/Lutino
Lutino	Green	Green	Green/Lutino
Lutino	Green/Lutino	Green Lutino	Lutino Green/Lutino
Lutino	Lutino	Lutino	Lutino**

*The color creamino can be substituted for lutino to find the results for two birds of the ground color blue.

**Breeding two red-eyed parents together is not considered a good practice. Your healthiest clutches with the highest percentages of lutino babies will come from the pairing of a lutino hen and a green split lutino cock.

Autosomal recessive: Both parents must carry the mutation, either visually or as a split, for it to show visually in progeny. Two birds split to an autosomal recessive color will have some babies of that color as well as babies that are their visual color. For example, a pair of white Fischer's split ino can have both white and albino babies. However, for sex-linked autosomal recessive mutations, such as lutino in peach-faced lovebirds, inheritance is as shown in the table above.

As you can see, if you put a hen who has a sex-linked recessive color with a cock who does not carry this color either visually or as a split, you will not get any babies that visually carry the color. However, all your males will be split to the sex-linked recessive color and can therefore pass it on to their daughters.

Peachfaced Lovebirds: Modes of Inheritance

Color	Mode of Inheritance
Green	Dominant
Blue	Autosomal recessive
Pied	Autosomal dominant
Ino (lutino or creamino)	Sex-linked recessive
Cinnamon	Sex-linked recessive
Dark Factors	Autosomal incomplete dominant
Violet Factors	Autosomal incomplete dominant
Whitefaced	Autosomal recessive
Orangefaced	Autosomal incomplete dominant

Masked Lovebirds: Modes of Inheritance

Color	Mode of Inheritance
Blue	Autosomal recessive
Dilute	Autosomal recessive
White	Autosomal recessive
Ino	Autosomal recessive
Dark Factors	Autosomal, codominant, incompletely dominant

Fischer's Lovebirds: Modes of Inheritance

Color	Mode of Inheritance
Blue	Autosomal recessive
Dilute	Autosomal recessive
Ino	Autosomal recessive
Yellow*	Autosomal recessive
Dark Factor	Autosomal, codominant, incompletely dominant
Violet Factor	Autosomal dominant

*A yellow/ino Fischer's results from the pairing of one ino parent and one yellow. These lovebirds are heterozygotic. They are yellow with black eyes. The overall color is more muted than seen in lutinos. Putting two yellow/ino Fischer's together will produce some lutino babies.

Modes of Inheritance

The tables above can guide you in determining how to pair parents to get the colors you would like in your babies. A number of other colors occur, but these are the most commonly bred in these species.

The modes of inheritance for Fischer's and masked are quite similar to those for other eye-ring species. Note that most mutations are auto-somal recessive, which means both parents must either visually show the mutation or carry it as a split for babies to show the mutation. Ino is not sex-linked in Fischer's or masked lovebirds.

This text has shown only the tip of the iceberg when it comes to the genetics of color inheritance in lovebirds. Many books are totally devoted to this topic. You are encouraged to do further reading if you plan to start a color breeding program.

Useful Addresses and Literature

Societies

African Lovebird Society
P.O. Box 142
San Marcos, CA 92079-0142
http://www.africanlovebirdsociety.
com

American Federation of Aviculture
P.O. Box 56218
Phoenix, AZ 85079-6218
http://www.afa.birds.org

Books

Coles, B. H. *Avian Medicine and Surgery.* Oxnard, UK: Blackwell Science Ltd., 1997.

D'Angieri, A. *The Colored Atlas of Lovebirds.* Neptune, NJ: T.F.H. Publications, Inc., 1997.

Forshaw, Joseph M. *Parrots of the World.* Neptune, NJ: T.F.H. Publications, Inc., 1973.

Ritchie, Branson. *Avian Viruses: Function and Control.* Lake Worth, FL: Wingers Publishing, Inc., 1995.

Periodicals

The AFA Watchbird
P.O. Box 56218
Phoenix, AZ 85079-6218

Bird Talk
P.O. Box 6050
Mission Viejo, CA 92690
http://www.birdtalk.com

Pet Bird Report
2236 Mariner Square Drive
PMB 35
Alameda, CA 94501
http://www.petbirdreport.com

Websites

About Guide to Pet Birds
http://birds.about.com

Parrot Parrot
http://www.parrotparrot.com

Index